# The Un-Bossy Boss

12 Powerful Questions to make YOU a Great Manager.

By

Gary Magenta

## Dedication

To my wife, Angela, thank you for making

everything wonderful in my life possible.

To Ian, having you as my son has simply

made me a better person.

To my son Jordan, you inspire me

by making everything look so easy.

# Contents

# Acknowledgements

A great accomplishment is best achieved with the help of others, and thus is the case for me. I have had the support of many people in the writing of this book. My family allowed me to lock myself away on weekends for 18 months. Thank you Angela, Ian and Jordan for your love and patience. My work family at Root Inc. has made it possible to bring this book to managers everywhere. My draft editor Veronica Hughes literally read the book to me, cover to cover, many times, so I could hear the way it sounded from the reader's perspective. Veronica is a true partner who was always honest with her commentary and sent me back to the keyboard when she thought I could do better. Thank you for your patience.

Tricia Richards, Lori Fournier and Adam Hastings provided their design talent, which has brought this book to life. Jason Stafne is the artist who, through his illustrations, has poignantly and often humorously captured the true meaning behind the book's many stories and dialogues. JJ Pastore is the gifted artist, friend and coachee who created the cover of this book.

Many people have read the seemingly never-ending iterations of this book and offered their comments, suggestions, and advice which can be seen throughout. Clients, co-workers, coaches, authors, family, friends, and neighbors all brought their contributions to this work. Jim Haudan graciously agreed to write the Foreword for this book and who paved the way for other authors at Root Inc. Rich Berens has been a great friend, manager and supporter. Mark Blankenship, Bill Carrier, Phil Hamburg, Jeff Lindeman, Michael Magenta, Karen Magenta, David Seltzer, Rex Soper and Rossaria Torriani all provided me with their insights and direction throughout the writing process. Thank you again to my wife, Angela, who in the writing process read this book more times than I did.

Dawn Ray and Toni Zoblotski provided their creative talents to help with the book and chapter titles, while Tim Hyatt's draft proofing showed me that there is a difference between the words "there and their," "here and hear" and "to and too." Margie Heck and Wanda Horn support me in my day-to-day work. They make all of my travel arrangements, keep my calendar, know all of my passwords, and have full access to my voicemail, email, and credit card accounts. With their help, I am able to work, coach others, play, and have time to write – thank you both!

I lost a great friend and employee for whom I tried to be a Great Manager. David Serdynski brought everything he had to his work. He shared his passion, emotion, and intellect with his clients, his co-workers, and with me, his manager. David, you are missed and I am happy to have had the chance to learn from you. Thank you.

I can recount my career thus far through relationships – relationships with people whom I have worked alongside, managed and those who have been my managers. Thank you to Arden Brion, Maria Forbes, Bruce Hulbert, Holly Jenkins, David Kalman, Robin Wooddall-Klein, Alison Lazenby, Don MacLean, Bryan Moon, Tracey Nawrocki, Brian Parsells, Christy Stone, Carl Wagner, Eliot Wajskol and Victor Zhang. These relationships have all helped mold and shape me and this book. I am grateful to all of you.

# Foreword

In many organizations today, the reality is that there are huge gaps between three groups of people: the leaders who can see what needs to be done but don't have their hands on the levers of change; the doers, who have their hands on the day-to-day levers of change but can't see the big picture; and managers, who are caught in the middle trying to interpret the strategy from their leaders and translate it into something meaningful that captures the hearts and minds of doers in the hopeful pursuit of better results.

Managers balance on a narrow strip between leaders and doers in most organizations, and their actions will determine if the organization's strategic dreams and aspirations come to life. They are the "meaning makers" who convert the intentions of the organization's strategic PowerPoint decks into the actions and behaviors of real people who must do something differently to actually improve performance.

Successful companies are those that can execute their strategies. Strategy without execution is meaningless. Execution without great managers is impossible. Managers are the critical variable in a successful business. People thrive under the guidance of a great manager or boss. They produce more, stay around longer, expect less, invest their discretionary effort voluntarily, and have a direct impact on profitability and performance.

Unfortunately, great bosses are more uncommon than common. Research shows that for every great boss, there are at least four with far less ability to motivate and inspire loyalty. The well-known career site Monster even identifies 21 types of bosses. Not surprisingly, 20 of the 21 are not the type of boss that any of us would want to work for. While the "clueless boss" immediately stands out on the list as one to avoid, so does the "buzzword boss," "bumbler boss," "buddy boss," and the "fearmonger boss."

Some individuals even take their frustration with their boss to new levels of creative expression. Consider 25-year-old Marina Shifrin's resignation, which really stood out. Her "I Quit" video went viral and in four days received over eight million views, as well as being shown on most morning and evening news shows. She hit a nerve with her creativity and message when she said that she works for an awesome company, but her boss only cares about quantity and not quality – so she was quitting. She also happened to dance out her video message to Kanye West's song "Gone."

Good bosses listen. Great bosses ask questions. Managers who become exceptional at the art of questioning actually become coaches to their teams. They possess the key skill of being able to talk less and authentically probe with a curious ear. The questions they ask help organize information, reframe problems, question the status quo, enable out-of-the-box thinking, and analyze critically – all with the intent to help the people they manage assess conflicts and opportunities in a way that enables them to arrive at the best solutions themselves.

The "best boss I ever had" is a statement that most of us have heard, reflected on, or engaged in a conversation about. The common denominator in this dialogue is the realization that we are mostly drawn to managers who know how to encourage, stretch, appreciate, understand, forgive, listen, enable, and assist us in our development to become more than we thought we were capable of becoming, while achieving more than we thought possible. It is the practical realization that the key to developing influential managers is to make other people feel good about themselves and their contributions, rather than to make them feel good about their manager.

Gary's book, *The Un-Bossy Boss*, shows managers exactly how to become the best boss we all wish we had. His approach ignites the realization in managers that they have tremendous power to change things, to influence people, to have a huge impact on the way in which people work, and to shape the environment most conducive for success. His focus on the 12 Powerful Questions to Make You a Great Manager represents the playbook to answer the question, "What exactly do the very best managers do?" Great bosses don't take. They give credit, confidence, support, guidance, and space for people to solve the most important business puzzles on their own. Gary gives us tremendous insight into the skills and practices at the heart of becoming the "Un-Bossy Boss," and his passion and belief in the transformative power of great managers has an inspirational impact on anyone who desires to unlock the true potential of their people.

Jim Haudan, CEO, Root Inc.

# Introduction: My Story

I was in my thirties when I took my first corporate job and began working under a manager. I had become an entrepreneur and independent restaurant owner in my mid-twenties after spending several years working in my parents' business, my friend's family business, and my wife's business. I had been working my entire life for successful people that I knew, loved, and respected, yet I never had a true manager. It was always difficult to think about the people who had forbidden me from watching TV on school nights, or asked me to pick up my socks, as managers or business role models.

When I sold my restaurant business and accepted a corporate position with a large hospitality-related distribution company, my plan was to work remotely for nine months from my home in Florida and then relocate to Illinois to take on a newly created position.

During the interview process, I met the man who would become my manager. I liked him; he was an affable, tenured vice president blessed with the gift of gab. But once I started with the company, I never heard from him. Never. I found this curious. Didn't he want to know what I was doing—or how I was doing it? Working 1,200 miles from the corporate office, I felt isolated, unsure, and very surprised that I was left to my own devices.

After three or four months of no communication, out of the blue, my manager called me from O'Hare Airport in Chicago. Finally! An opportunity to get feedback and ask questions. That, however, was not the case. "Gary," he said briskly, "your cell phone bill is way too high. Please be sure you reduce the cost moving forward." I said, "Okay," to which he quickly replied, "I'm running to catch a plane. Talk to you soon."

That was the entire call. I told myself that he was very busy, and I'd have plenty of time to talk with him when I got to Illinois; I was nonetheless deflated. Even though I was working independently, I had ideas and a list of things I wanted to accomplish when I moved to the corporate office.

With a glow of excitement, I reported to work on a Monday morning in July, almost a year after starting with the company. After spending the weekend moving my young family across the country, I was still bursting with enthusiasm as I walked into my manager's office at 8:00 a.m.

He looked up at me, surprised. "What are you doing here?" he said. "Is this the week you're starting at corporate? I forgot and, um, I don't think we have an office set up for you yet. Ask my secretary to find you somewhere to sit until we can get you set up." With that he dismissed me without further discussion.

The only thing worse than his welcome was his reaction later that day as he reviewed the raise I was supposed to receive with my relocation. "We agreed to pay you what? That's more than the other guys in the department make! This is going to be awkward for me."

I left his office, found an open phone, and called my wife. I told her that I thought we had made a big mistake. This was my first day in my new office, the beginning of a new position, and I was already having doubts. This was no way to start a new job! First, my manager forgot I was moving across the country, and now he was balking about the pay he had promised. I asked myself, is this a bad joke, or some sort of a hazing process? Was I being tested? No, this was real. I couldn't help but wonder, if my manager was representative of the whole company, what else could I expect?

Over the next few months, whenever I had the rare chance to meet with my manager, he alone talked through the meeting. He was always multitasking—talking, typing, and answering his phone at the same time. I had little (if any) opportunity to share my thoughts and ideas. He never once asked me how my family was adjusting or what I thought about the work. What he did was talk and talk and talk about the deals he was closing and the people he knew and the good old days. He was like a television that I couldn't shut off.

I was frustrated. Why hadn't he talked about what was important to me? What about the questions I had? What about my ideas on how we could improve our business and the work I was doing? I wanted his input, feedback, recognition, and counsel. I needed direction on where to focus my time and energy. I thought I was taking the right actions and getting good results, but how could I be sure without any feedback? His lack of interest in my work, or in me personally, was impacting my performance. I was on my own, and I had no idea how I was measuring up. I couldn't see how my work was contributing to the team or the company.

Something needed to change.

I'd wait outside his office to catch him leaving for a meeting, or going to the men's room. I'd follow him, talking about things that were important to me and that I believed to be important to the business. After about five months, I waited by his office late one night, lurking in the shadows like some kind of corporate stalker, and as he left for the parking lot, I appeared at his side and walked with him the entire way, talking a mile a minute to get out everything I had to say.

I hadn't considered that there was a right and a wrong time for this conversation. Because I felt neglected all the time, I was focused on somehow commanding some of his time and attention. I told him that I didn't feel I was being heard, and that I had a lot to offer. He said, "Look, if you want to talk about something that's important to you, do not follow me into the men's room. Do not follow me to my car when I'm going home because I'm probably not hearing what you have to say at times like that."

I said, "That's great advice, and in the future I'll be sure to ask you if it's a good time to talk." Never one to give up, I asked, "So—when would be a good time to talk?" This was his answer: "Well, there's not going to be a good time to talk because I'm leaving the company for another job."

What?

So ended my first experience with a "manager." While I believed (and still do) that he was not a very good manager or role model, he did start me thinking about what kind of manager I had been to my

past employees, what kind of manager I wanted to become, and how I would like my future managers to engage me.

I decided that I wanted to have a manager—and be a manager—who treated people with respect, who valued them as real human beings with meaningful lives and valuable experiences that extended beyond the halls of business. In the ensuing years, I've observed and worked with what I call Great Managers, those who have learned to bring out the best in their employees so they can reach their full potential and contribution to the business. I've also had the benefit of managing others who have taught me a great deal on my continuing journey to become a great manager myself. I'm grateful for the opportunity to share what I've learned in the past 25 years, and I hope you find it valuable on your road to becoming a truly great manager yourself.

# Chapter 1

## The Dawn of the Great Manager

For years, I've worked with major corporations and their leadership teams in North America and Europe to engage their employees in business issues from strategy to customer service. I find that most companies have a real appreciation for the development of their top leaders, as well as for the people who stand on the front lines of their businesses.

> *No matter how intelligent the leader, how exceptional the plan, or how robust the training, change can be attained and sustained only when a Great Manager is in place.*

Countless books have been written on leadership, and an incalculable amount of money has been spent on training those who interact with customers directly. Yet I've found that no matter how intelligent the leader, how exceptional the plan, or how robust the training, organizational change can be attained and sustained only when Great Managers are in place. I'm not talking about *any* managers. When I say Great Managers, I mean those who employ the techniques that you're about to discover.

In this book we will explore time-tested, real-world methods of management that will, if properly applied, elevate your management skills to new heights, and produce measurable and profitable results for your company.

The fact is that today, successful managers must be more than just order-givers. They must learn to engage those they are managing in human terms. They must become coaches. Not coaches with a whistle, yelling at the team, but coaches with insight and compassion, wisdom and patience, who bring out the best in those they manage. The manager who understands this, and who gains the necessary skills, will become a Great Manager.

Here you will learn a coaching model I call ASK, an acronym for **A**lign, **S**eek, and **K**ickstart, all of which will be covered in much greater detail as we go along. The ASK coaching model inspires managers to go beyond simply telling their employees what to do and how to do it. The ASK coaching model helps any manager become a Great Manager by bringing out the best in their employees. The secret to doing so lies in asking a series of Powerful Questions of themselves and their employees.

These Powerful Questions are easy to learn and remember. They cover the six spheres of influence that impact an employee's performance: **J**udgments, **A**ttitude, **S**peech, **P**hysicality, **A**ctions, and **R**esults—known collectively as JASPAR. In subsequent chapters we will explore in detail each component of JASPAR, and see how asking Powerful Questions that target the six spheres of influence will bring out the best in both you and your employees, and help you become a Great Manager.

But first let's explore our definitions of a Great Manager and take a look at some of the pitfalls and false beliefs that accompany the position of manager in today's business environment. In other words, what's working, and what's not?

The difference between a manager and a Great Manager lies in the ways in which they interact with their employees. Great Managers see themselves as CEOs—Chief *Engagement* Officers—of their departments or functions, and especially of their teams. They view their primary role as connecting organizational goals to the individual skills and capabilities of their team members so they can drive business results. Great Managers must know their employees as *real people* and tap into the strengths, desires, and goals of each person in order to help them deliver the desired results to the business while creating satisfaction for themselves.

When I meet with corporate leaders about deploying new strategies or initiatives, I always ask about the capability of their managers to deploy and sustain the changes needed to achieve those initiatives. The most common reply is this: "They're *managers*. They should already know how to do that!" They should? Based on what?

Although this may be conventional corporate thinking, it continues to puzzle me. In most organizations, managers are people who were once great individual contributors, and as a result, have been rewarded with a promotion that is focused on leading others. The vast majority are not trained, equipped, or prepared to lead teams or deliver results through other people. They're great employees who have now been promoted to manager. They are then left alone to define what being a manager means. Is it any wonder that if an organization has 100 managers, there may be 100 different definitions of what a manager does?

Although promoting an outstanding individual contributor to manager is a common step in the business world, it's *not* a natural progression in terms of skill and ability. As a matter of fact, what's required of a manager is often diametrically opposed to what's required of an employee. As a great employee, your job is to give the best you have to offer. As a Great Manager, in addition to giving the best you have to offer, your job is to bring out the best that *others* have to offer.

A dictionary defines "manager" as "one who handles, controls, or directs." Handles? Controls? Directs? I've never wanted to be handled, controlled, or directed. Have you? Those words are about *telling people what to do* . . . the outdated management style of "yelling and telling." Where are the words that focus on *coaching* and *developing* the people who are the heart and soul of any business?

## What's a Manager's Real Job?
Managers are often pulled in a thousand directions. They're expected to implement new corporate initiatives, work with clients, conduct daily business operations, track metrics, and recruit and manage employees. However, for the Great Manager, these duties are only a part of what leads to success. Great Managers believe that coaching and developing their people is their number one job. However, often times when managers are asked to prioritize their responsibilities, coaching their employees comes last. In order for any business to succeed, and for managers to triumph, companies need to rely on their teams to deliver the desired results. At the same time, employees rely on Great Managers to inform, coach, and develop them. The execution of this unspoken contract between a manager and an employee is what sets Great Managers apart from an average manager. The managers who deliver exceptional results through their employees represent the best of the best, the top tier of managers: *they all have the ability to coach their teams and the individuals on them.*

> *Great Managers bring out the best in their employees, who, at their best, turn customers into fans.*

## The Great Manager's Effect on Business Success

Without Great Managers, a business may survive, but it will not thrive. Today, Great Managers are a necessary competitive advantage. Great Managers bring out the best in their employees, who, at *their* best, turn customers into fans. Employees who are at their best are those who are most equipped to engage their customers, building loyalty and greater profitability. Consider the fact that managers have a multiplier effect on their businesses. If a manager has five employees and each employee interacts with 10 customers, the shadow of that manager falls on 50 customers. Those 50 customers may each influence 10 or more potential customers; the numbers can become huge in a short time.

Many companies have multiple divisions and locations driving toward a common goal. Their managers are required to create results that contribute to these goals, and often today they must achieve those results with far fewer people. As a result, maximizing the contribution of every employee is more critical than ever. This requires an entirely new kind of a manager—a Great Manager.

Are Great Managers born that way, or can they be trained? The answer is both! For some, it comes quite naturally, while others learn from role models, experience, training, hard work, and practice. Regardless of your role models, or whether you coach and manage intuitively or need training, don't worry; by reading this book, you are taking an important step toward becoming a Great Manager.

## The Wake-Up Call

Organizations are realizing the importance and impact Great Managers can have on their businesses. They're starting to invest in building the skills of managers to become coaches and developers of successful people. This should be seen as a wake-up call for old-school managers. For them, the future may be bleak, but for those who want to coach and develop people—Great Managers—their time has arrived. Just as businesses must meet the changing needs of customers, managers must meet the needs of an ever-changing workforce.

A 2011 study by Bersin & Associates ("High-Impact Performance Management") showed that 70% of organizations claim they coach their employees but admit that many managers lack coaching skills. In addition, the study says that only 11% of senior leaders actively coach others. Those who do are three times more effective at producing results. (If senior leaders aren't role-modeling coaching, it's likely that managers down the line aren't either.)

At the heart of these statistics lies a manager's ability to engage and connect with teams and individuals on issues that are critical to business results. Great Managers have a powerful, positive impact on an organization's success, and that translates to the performance and retention of its employees.

Many managers have been told (and still believe) that they need to have all the answers, solve all the problems, and *tell* their employees how to implement *their* solutions. Managers *tell* people, "Here's what needs to be done, and this is the way I want you to do it." Later, they merely check in to ensure that their instructions were followed correctly and *tell* people, if necessary, how to improve or adjust in order to meet their expectations.

| | |
|---|---|
| **Believe they** need to have all the answers | **Help** employees find the answers |
| **Present** solutions | **Co-create** solutions with employees |
| **Tell** employees what to do | **Coach and develop** employees |
| **Ensure** that **their** instructions are followed | **Discover** employees' passions and knowledge |
| **Tell** employees how to improve | **Value** employees' experience in and out of the workplace in order to help them **maximize their contribution** |

## What Does a Great Manager Do?

The approach of merely yelling and telling isn't practiced by Great Managers who engage employees in genuine conversations, tapping into their passions, knowledge, and experience.

*Great Managers know to ask Powerful Questions.* This is the primary difference between a manager and Great Manager.

*Great Managers are active listeners, offer observations, and enable shifts in beliefs, actions, and behaviors.* They do this so employees can discover their own solutions, challenges, and opportunities.

*Great Managers value and harness employees' experience from inside and outside of the workplace, regarding them as "whole peo-*

*ple.*" These are the tools that a Great Manager uses to help employees create and implement their own solutions.

***Great Managers engage employees in creating the solutions they'll be asked to implement*** – as opposed to *telling* them. This is essential and somewhat counter to commonly practiced management techniques. Employees are much more likely to implement and use solutions that they take part in crafting. If employees are expected to be accountable, make decisions, and be effective stewards of businesses, they need to participate in the solutions that they're responsible for carrying out. The job of a Great Manager is to involve, motivate, and coach employees through this process.

***Great Managers ensure that the team has the necessary skills, capabilities, and tools for whatever challenges or opportunities the marketplace presents.*** Frontline employees have their hands on the levers of change, and in many cases, directly on products, services, and customers. In order for a business to thrive, its employees must be quick to respond to the demands of a new and evolving marketplace.

In the future a manager may not even hold the title of "manager." Perhaps "coach" or "people developer" will be more appropriate. This new-and-improved approach will be rewarded with the greatest contribution an employee can give – their discretionary effort, serving a company with their heads, hearts, and minds.

### Are You Ready to Be Great?

What's holding managers back from being great? When I went directly to managers to find out, I discovered two common themes:

    **Gary:** What's holding you back from coaching your employees?

    **Manager:** I don't have the time.

    **Gary:** What else?

**Manager:** I don't know how! What do I say?

**Gary:** If you knew what to say and how to coach your employees, would you find the time?

**Manager:** Of course I would!

Let's be honest; it's not about time; we're *all* time deprived! It's about competence, capability, and comfort. You can actually *save* time by having coaching conversations. You just need to know how.

For many managers, coaching conversations are painful, and human beings will do almost anything to avoid pain. In an effort to avoid the potential misery of having coaching conversations when they feel ill equipped, most steer clear of it altogether. "I'm too busy" becomes the story that managers tell themselves about why they don't coach employees.

Promise yourself now that you'll never do this again! Take the Gary Pledge and repeat after me:

"I, (state your name), will never again use the excuse of being too busy to get out of coaching my employees."

### Don't Let the Past Get in the Way

Many managers learn to manage through observation—as in parenting, there is no handbook for bringing out the best in others. Some organizations may offer management training, but for too many managers, their only source of information comes directly from their *past* managers. Think about your own management style. How have your previous managers influenced you?

You may be intentionally including some of your previous managers' methods with your employees, or you may be doing it unconsciously. If you've had a manager who was comfortable and proficient at coaching you, then you may have already had a good foundation for how and when to have coaching conversations. However, if you're like most, the concept of coaching will be new to you. In either case, together we'll explore methods and tools that will help you become a Great Manager.

## Great Managers Need Great Beliefs

The road to being a Great Manager begins with the adoption of this set of beliefs. Great Managers believe:

- In the *power and potential* of individual employees.
- That their primary role is that of *coach and developer of people.*
- That coaching is both *formal and informal.*
- That *knowing the right questions to ask* is more important than having all the answers.
- That their *relationship with employees* is a critical measure of their employees' job satisfaction.
- That their success is measured by the *success of their employees.*

As a Great Manager, soft skills are even more important than hard skills because they enable the manager to engage an employee and create trust. Hard skills are more technical or procedure-based by nature and generally easy to measure, while soft skills, also known as people skills, are difficult to quantify. Soft skills are more relationship-based; they focus on communication and require the ability to

> "[M]any organizations are failing to leverage the role of middle managers in stimulating engagement. These people have a critical role to play in influencing, engaging, and empowering teams. People leave organizations that have not properly equipped managers to be engaging. Managers could and should have a positive impact on employee engagement."
>
> From an Aon Hewitt report published in HR Magazine (UK edition) October 2011.

coach and create a two-way dialogue with individuals and teams. Your ability to coach and build strong relationships with employees will lead to higher employee engagement, greater satisfaction, increased productivity, and lower turnover. These outcomes can only be achieved by a manager who invests in building their soft skills.

You're probably proficient in the hard skills of your business: systems, equipment, software, contracts, products, and other components that support sales or operations. It's also likely that this expertise was a significant factor in your being hired into your position.

Possessing exceptional hard skills in the absence of soft skills may indicate that you're an excellent individual contributor with a manager title, but you're not really a manager, and certainly not a Great Manager . . . yet.

The dawn of the Great Manager is *now*.

## Worksheet for Chapter 1
## The Dawn of the Great Manager

1.  The type of manager you are today was probably influenced by the managers you've worked for in years past. Think back to the best manager you ever had. What were some qualities of that manager that you admired and that you would like to demonstrate with your employees?

    **Qualities I want to demonstrate:**

    •

    •

    •

2.  Now, think about a manager who might not have been at their best when you were working together. What were some traits that they demonstrated that you never want to repeat?

    **Traits not to be repeated:**

    •

    •

    •

3. In Chapter 1, we started to explore why Great Managers are so important and considered some of the things they do that distinguish them from ordinary managers. In addition to what we have already discovered, what *one thing* do you believe all Great Managers have in common?

4. As you think about how you manage today, what are you most proud of? What would you change or improve for your benefit and that of your employees?

| Most Proud of | Improve or Change |
| --- | --- |
| • | • |
| • | • |
| • | • |

5. What, if anything, is holding you back from being a truly Great Manager?

# Chapter 2

## Don't Yell and Tell:
## An Introduction to Coaching

When I was a young manager, I dreaded giving feedback to my employees. The idea of coaching them was completely foreign to me. Giving feedback felt the same as having a confrontation and the thought of it would literally keep me up at night. It was so daunting that I often put it off, waiting until my frustration boiled over.

I'd complain about someone's performance to others; I'd go home and tell my wife. But taking the feedback directly to my employees happened *only* when I got mad enough to yell at them and tell them I wasn't happy. Looking back, I can only imagine their surprise at my outbursts. After all, I wasn't managing mind-readers! If I hadn't told them, how could they have known I was unhappy with their performance for days, weeks, and sometimes even months?

Giving feedback and input on performance can be a manager's greatest gift to an employee, but no one wants a gift thrown at their head. In my early days as a manager, I was throwing quite a few gifts—yelling—and my employees had to duck—a lot.

I will never forget the first time I decided to fire someone. The night before I had planned to let him go, I couldn't sleep; I was incredibly nervous about delivering the message. The next morning as I prepared for work I literally felt nauseated thinking about letting him go. I justified my decision by telling myself that I had repeatedly given him the feedback he needed and that he refused to change. In retrospect, I can see that there is no way he could have interpreted my yelling as feedback.

With that in mind, I'd like to take a moment to apologize.

> *Dear employees from my beginning days as a manager,*
> *I'm sorry for yelling and telling. I didn't know any better at the time.*
> *Sincerely,*
> *Gary*

## Taking the First Step

As we saw in Chapter 1, we all want to be involved in conversations where we can discuss our opinions, thoughts, ideas, concerns, ambitions, and challenges—where we can vet, plan, form ideas, and develop solutions. Yet our history, education, government, and business world have, in large part, bred managers who yell and tell. Managers struggle to connect to their people as individuals; they fail to maximize the contribution and potential of every person on their team. This often results in managers who under-deliver to their employees, teams, businesses, and their own careers.

In order to be a Great Manager, you need to be an effective coach with the ability to ask Powerful Questions, listen actively, offer observations. You must help your employee create the shifts in their beliefs and actions that will result in the achievement of desired results. Coaching is a *partnership* between the coach and the employee, where the main goal is to help the employee develop and contribute to the business.

The first step in great coaching is to understand that all people have their own judgments, opinions, or views. All these assessments—good or bad, difficult or easy, fair or unfair, possible or impossible, wrong or right—are subjective and are determined by the person doing the observing. Our observations are based on our own experience and how we listen, view, and interpret a situation. Things are never exactly the way one person or another views them. One person may think that fast food is unappealing, while another sees it as their guilty pleasure. As a Great Manager and coach, your job will be to understand the view of *all your employees.*

## A Philosophy of Coaching

> *A Great Manager is a partner of employees and teams, helping them to come to their own conclusions, take action, and reach their potential.*

Great Managers have the ability to drive uncommonly successful results for their organization by coaching their people. Coaching is based on the premise that, with help, people can ignite their own potential and achieve or even accelerate their results by discovering solutions for themselves. Coaches help people identify their individual aspirations for change, desired results, and solutions and then match those goals with the needs of the business. A coach doesn't just dole out advice or act as an expert. Great Managers and coaches know that, although employees may outwardly agree with their leaders' conclusions, they will ultimately take action based on their own beliefs. Therefore, a Great Manager is a partner of employees and teams, helping them to come to their own conclusions, take action, and reach their potential.

If you're new to the philosophy of coaching, you may need to make a shift from telling, giving advice and answers, into asking Powerful Questions that allow your people to discover solutions for themselves. As you do this, remember that your employees will also need to make the same shifts. Some may still ask for advice and answers to their dilemmas. When you are coaching an employee—even if you believe you have the best ideas—don't just give answers or advice. Ask questions to help your employees reach their own conclusions.

At the start, this shift may prove challenging for everyone. When taking on this new managing method, share your approach with your team. Describe how you'd like to involve them and what you expect of them. They may look at you quizzically; explain your role as a partner and coach who will help them discover answers. Show them how this will benefit them, the team, and the business. Be sure they know that this partnership will work only with their full participation.

**The Guiding Principles of Coaching**
With the philosophy of coaching established, you'll need some guiding principles to use as your roadmap to becoming a Great Manager—your foundation for coaching. These principles apply to almost any business results you hope to achieve. And don't be surprised if you find yourself using them in your personal life too!

**1. Establish the right time to talk.**
You can't coach an employee if the time isn't right. Always ask, "Is this a good time to talk?" Employees may have the time, but may also have other things on their minds that will keep them from fully participating at a given moment. *The right conversation at the wrong time always becomes the wrong conversation.* As a Great Manager, you may be anxious or excited about wanting to talk to an employee.

By making sure that the time is right, you'll help ensure that the conversation is effective and productive.

## 2. Ask Powerful Questions.

Asking—rather than telling—offers employees the opportunity to think independently and discover their own solutions. Asking Powerful Questions is the first step in finding out what is most important to people. They are also the questions that help your employees effectively challenge themselves and generate productive ideas and thus productive performance. My years of working with managers and teams have shown me that asking questions—and therefore engaging employees in a two-way dialogue—is far more effective than simply telling them what to do. The additional benefit is that once your employees start to understand the impact of Powerful Questions, they will learn to ask these questions of themselves, and eventually of others.

## 3. Look, listen, and follow your intuition.

The words that employees use are only part of the stories they're telling. Their gestures, tone of voice, emotions, and even what they are *not* saying can be equally important. Listen, but also use your intuition to understand the whole story. The information and impressions you gather will lead to more Powerful Questions and greater observations to share with your employees.

## 4. Check for understanding and clarity.

Never presume that you understand everything an employee tells you, and don't rely solely on your intuition. As a Great Manager and coach, check your understanding by summarizing what you heard and sharing your hunches. Ask if your conclusions are correct, and ask for clarification when it's needed.

### 5. Offer your observations and create shifts.

The ability to help your employees shift their thinking is the difference between merely having a conversation and having a *coaching* conversation. Creating a shift is the defining moment of any coaching conversation, the clarifying moment when your employee can see possibilities that weren't apparent just moments earlier. Ask,  "May I offer you my observations?" in order to facilitate those shifts. With permission, share key observations—what you observed about their judgments, attitude, speech, and physicality (their body language). These insights often lead to shifts in one or all of these areas.

### 6. Brainstorm solutions and actions.

As a partner on this journey to new management practices with your employee or team, you can help brainstorm solutions based on the new insights. These may include offering your observations, suggestions, and support. If so, remember that any suggestion is just that—an idea or a hint, not an answer or a mandate. The purpose of brainstorming is to help people come to their own conclusions and establish the actions they'll take. Keep an open mind and stay flexible about what develops as a result of brainstorming solutions.

### It's All in How You Look at It

 We all know that the actions we take create our results. As a coach, you can help people see that their actions are based on their judgments about situations and what they believe the outcomes will be. You can also show them that they have the power to shift those judgments.

To see how our judgments can influence our attitudes, speech, physicality, actions, and eventually, our results, consider this story:

With brown-bag lunches in hand, Lorna and Meredith head to the picnic tables outside their office. They desperately want to escape their windowless cubicles and enjoy the outdoors. Once outside, Lorna turns to Meredith, and with excitement in her voice, exclaims, "What a beautiful day! It's perfect out here!" Meredith squints at the ground, hunches her shoulders, and says, "It's too hot. I hate the heat! I'm disappointed. I was really looking forward to eating outside today."

So, is it a beautiful day, or is it too hot? Based on the individual judgments of Lorna and Meredith, it's neither or it's both, and two very different actions followed. Lorna, with a spring in her step, grabbed her laptop and worked outside for the rest of the afternoon. Meredith sluggishly made her way back inside and ate at her cubicle. She was disappointed at the prospect of being indoors all day instead of spending time outside as she had wanted.

When we dissect Lorna's and Meredith's results, we see six separate spheres of influence:

**Lorna:**
- Judgment = It's "a beautiful day!"
- Attitude = Excitement
- Speech = "It's perfect out here!"
- Physicality = Spring in her step, excitement in her voice
- Actions = Takes her laptop outside
- Results = Spends the afternoon working outdoors being productive

**Meredith:**
- Judgment = "It's too hot!"
- Attitude = Disappointment
- Speech = "I hate the heat!"
- Physicality = Eyes down, shoulders slouched, sluggish
- Actions = Returns to her windowless cubicle
- Results = Eats lunch at her desk, spends the afternoon inside and not working at her best

What if Meredith had focused on the end result she wanted—to spend time outside? Let's imagine that Lorna had asked her this question: "Meredith, how can you beat the heat and still spend time outside today?" What possibilities might become available to Meredith? She might find a nice shade tree to sit under, sip lemonade to keep cool, or wait to go out a bit later when the heat subsided.

This is exactly the process that a Great Manager can use when working with an employee. The Great Manager asks Powerful Questions to uncover employees' **judgments**, and then helps them shift their **attitude**, **speech**, **physicality**, and ultimately the **actions** they take and the **results** they achieve. These six spheres of influence are the framework of the JASPAR coaching model, which we'll explore thoroughly in Chapter 5.

Read on!

## Worksheet for Chapter 2
## Don't Yell and Tell: Introduction to Coaching

1.  Think of a time when a boss, colleague, or friend coached you on an important topic or issue. What did it feel like to have someone invest in you in that way? If you've never had an experience like this, what would it mean to you to have one?

2.  As you consider the idea of coaching each person on your team to maximize their contribution and potential, what excites you most? If you have any concerns, what are they?

| What Excites Me Most about Coaching | My Concerns about Coaching |
|---|---|
| • | • |
| • | • |
| • | • |

3.  Which of the six Guiding Principles of Coaching are already part of the way you engage your employees? Which ones are you anxious to learn more about?

| I Already Follow These Principles | I Want To Learn More About These Principles |
|---|---|
| • | • |
| • | • |
| • | • |

4. We know that the actions we take create the results we get. As you consider incorporating coaching into the way you manage, what results do you hope to create for yourself, your individual employees, your team, and your organization?

# Chapter 3

## The 12 Powerful Questions

As my own skills grew, I evolved my yell and tell management style into something that I now refer to as "cheerleader management." Although I couldn't do splits or back flips, I began to vigorously cheer on my employees; loud and proud. I'd tell them, "You can do it!," "I believe in you!," "You're the best!," and other such terms of encouragement. There's nothing wrong with encouragement, but shouting positive phrases is still yelling and telling—it just uses nicer words. If you fall into the "cheerleader management" category, put down the pompoms and unleash your employees' potential by picking up Powerful Questions.

Unleashing the potential of individual employees and teams requires powerful coaching skills, including the ability to ask Powerful Questions. These questions don't just evoke answers—they engage employees in critical thinking. They allow people to be part of creating their own solutions. To encourage critical thinking, for example, try asking yourself, "If you were looking in on this conversation, what advice would you give yourself?"

**The Benefits of Powerful Questions**

Powerful Questions will help you to be a Great Manager in several valuable ways. First, these questions are designed to provide you with a complete picture, instead of just one limited angle. Powerful Questions are your keys to uncovering judgments and motivation for feelings, words, and physicality in the workplace. These questions will help reveal the actions that employees are taking or want to take, the decision-making processes behind their actions, and the results that they hope to achieve.

When asked effectively and answered honestly, Powerful Questions help employees to reach their own conclusions and discover how they can best support, contribute, and deliver results for the business, for the team, and for themselves. Also, the dialogue that

> *Powerful Questions allow you to find out what's important to employees and connect that to the goals of the business for the benefit of both.*

Powerful Questions create generate trust and reinforces the relationships between you and your employees. It provides an opportunity to learn what's important to them and enables employees to connect their goals to the goals of the business for the benefit of both parties involved. Powerful Questions are also catalysts, and their real potency is in the conversations they generate. As a Great Manager, your most significant role is coaching. Asking Powerful Questions is the best way to have consistently successful coaching conversations.

Let's compare . . .

Here are two performance-based dialogues that show how two managers might handle an identical situation. Consider which manager is effectively building a relationship, establishing trust, and connecting the employee's personal goals with those of the business.

The employee and manager work in a large call center. The performance of this employee has been in decline for several months. In the past this employee has performed very well in his role at the help desk, but recently the manager noticed the employee has been coming in late and leaving early. He reviews this employee's performance metrics, and listens to some customer calls the employee has been handling. The manager notices a sharp decline in the employee's response time and attitude. The manager knows he must talk to the employee about these performance gaps.

## How a *Manager* Works
The manager approaches the employee at his open cubicle:

**Manager:** Your performance hasn't been up to par. You've been taking way too long to get your work done. You're not meeting your goals, and you've been coming in late and leaving early. Do you understand what I'm talking about?

**Employee:** I guess so.

**Manager:** I need to see some improvement in your work, or we're going to have a more serious conversation. I expect you to stick to our normal work hours and do a better job of satisfying our customers who call the help desk. Do you have any questions?

**Employee:** I'll work on it, but I . . .

**Manager:** Look, I know you're capable and I just need you to make the changes, okay?

**Employee:** Umm . . . okay, I'll do better.

**Manager:** Thanks. I know you will.

## How a *Great Manager* Works

**Great Manager:** Do you have some time to talk?

**Employee:** Yeah sure, what's up?

**Great Manager:** I just want to check in with you. Let's take a walk to the break room and grab a cup of coffee.

**Employee:** All right, let me find someone to cover my calls and I'll meet you there in a few minutes.

Once the two meet in the break room they sit down at a small table in the corner where the manager is sure that no one can hear their conversation.

**Manager:** I've noticed some changes in your work and I wanted to check in with you. How do you think things are going?

**Employee:** Ah, not so good right now.

**Manager:** I hope I can help; what's up?

**Employee:** Our new system is really stressing me out! Using the new technology is taking me twice as long to resolve my customers' issues.

**Great Manager:** New technology can take time to learn. What else?

**Employee:** Well, my dad's been sick, so I've had to juggle work and taking care of him and that's been exhausting.

**Great Manager:** I'm sorry to hear about your dad. Are you taking care of him yourself, or do you have anyone who's helping you?

**Employee:** My brother lives out of state, and my mom has passed, so it is basically just me.

**Great Manager:** You've got a lot going on right now. How's this been affecting you?

**Employee:** Oh boy! Well, I've completely given up my social life, and I can barely get to work on time, let alone master a new system and give my customers great service.

**Great Manager:** I'd like to help. What if we spent the rest of our time brainstorming how you can get your performance back on track and make sure you can still take care of your dad?

**Employee:** Thanks, that works for me!

Which dialogue will yield the best results, build trust, and ultimately garner this employee's full and best effort? The benefits of choosing the second dialogue over the first are clear. This is the type of effective dialogue you'll be able to achieve by asking Powerful Questions.

This Great Manager used Powerful Questions as opposed to telling, and was able to get at the core of the employee's problem. Unlike the first example, where the manager didn't learn anything at all about the real issues, the second conversation leaves the manager and employee ready to make progress, and discover solutions that will make a difference.

### What Makes a Question Powerful?
Powerful Questions have four characteristics:

**They're open-ended:** They can't be answered with just a yes, no, or any other single word. They are designed to elicit thoughtful answers based on your employees' knowledge and emotions.

**They're non-judgmental:** Powerful Questions aren't leading and are devoid of your personal opinions or standards, so employees feel free to share their own views.

**They're provocative:** They challenge thinking and probe for answers that your employee may have never thought existed. Questions that generate new thoughts can easily lead to new conclusions, actions, and results.

**They're respectful:** When you're considerate of your employees' feelings and emotions, they feel appreciated and are more apt to answer honestly.

The following chart shows the difference between "traditional" questions and powerful ones:

| | Is it OPEN-ENDED? | Is it RESPECTFUL? | Is it PROVOCATIVE? | Is it NON-JUDGMENTAL? | Is it POWERFUL? |
|---|---|---|---|---|---|
| Do you see what you did wrong with that customer? | | | | | NO |
| How can you do a better job with that customer next time? | ✓ | ✓ | ✓ | | NO |
| What did you notice about the interaction with that customer? | ✓ | ✓ | ✓ | ✓ | YES! |

**The Best Powerful Questions**

Powerful Questions don't need to be complex. In fact, simple questions often carry the most impact. I've provided my favorites in a framework I call ASK:

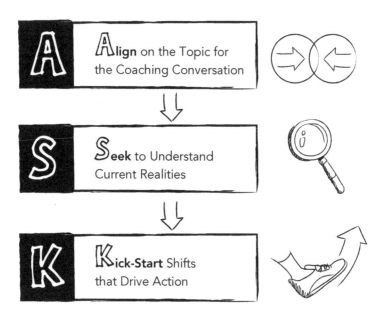

The order of the questions in the ASK framework is a guide that you can follow. You'll determine which questions apply to each conversation, tailoring them to fit your needs.

**ALIGN on the topic for the coaching conversation:**
- What is *most important* for you to talk about?
- What are your *desired results*?
- What are your *actual results* today, and how did they come to be?

**SEEK to understand current realities, real or perceived:**
- What's really happening, and what are the *judgments* you added to your story?

- What *attitude* or outlook do you have based on your judgments?
- What *speech* or words are you using, and how are they impacting your ability to achieve the results you want?
- How are your judgments and attitudes showing up *physically*?

**KICK-START shifts that drive action:**
- What *actions* will your current thinking (judgments, attitude, speech, or physicality) likely inspire?
- If nothing were in your way, and you knew that everything would turn out well, what would you do?
- May I offer you my *observations*?
- What *new practices* can you put into place to ensure your success?
- Are you willing to *take action*? By when? If not, why not?

**The bonus question:**
- *What else?*

Let's further explore each of these.

**What is most important for you to talk about?**
Finding out what is number 1 in the mind of an employee is a priority. Whatever subject is important to them should become important to you, too. Remember, employees bring their whole selves to work. What's most important for them to talk about may have nothing to do with their work, but it may directly impact their performance. Likewise, you will want to raise topics that are important for you to discuss with your employee. Make sure that you are creating a two-way conversation by checking for understanding and uncovering their point of view and co-creating an action plan if needed.

> *Encouraging employees to articulate their desired results empowers them to establish goals that they can own.*

## What are your desired results?

Asking employees about their desired results encourages them to consider what they want and what's expected of them. Encouraging employees to articulate their desired results empowers them to establish goals that they can own. Once you, as the coach, understand your employees' desired results, you can help them shape goals that will support their success.

## What are your actual results today, and how did they come to be?

Your employees need to understand where they are starting from and what results they're actually getting. From this vantage point, an employee can identify gaps to be bridged between actual and desired results. This question allows each party to gain insight into what the employee believes are their contributions. This question can be very revealing—employees may begin talking about things that they believe have held them back. As a Great Manager, it's your job to pay particular attention to this part of the conversation, because it can often confirm or identify the need to revisit what is actually most important to talk about.

## What's really happening, and what are the judgments you added to your story?

Coaching your employee requires you to help them separate the facts from their judgments or views. Listen carefully and distinguish facts that can be differentiated from judgments that are subjective. Your employee might even regard their judgments as beliefs. Your job is to help your employee understand the difference.

**What attitude or outlook do you have based on your judgments?**
An employee's judgments influence their attitude. Evaluating attitude and outlook helps employees recognize the lens they view any given situation through and how that perspective might be impacting their ability to achieve their desired results. More often than not, becoming aware of the attitude is a revelation for your employee and can often be eye opening for you as their manager. You may witness a true "aha" moment when an employee realizes for the first time that achieving the desired results may require a shift or adjustment on their part.

> *An employee will realize that achieving the desired results may require a shift on their part.*

**What words are you using, and how are they impacting your ability to achieve the results you want?**
Listen carefully to the speech an employee uses to describe current results, attitude, and judgments. Listen for *thinking words, feeling words,* and *tone of voice,* which can help or hinder their ability to achieve their goals. Often times your employee will not even be conscious of the words or tone they are using and the impact they are having on their ability to achieve their desired results. As a Great Manager, part of your job is to highlight the speech that may be negatively affecting their outcomes and of course reinforcing that which is helpful. When an employee is made aware of their speech and tone, they can better see the impact it has on their actions, results, and the people around them.

**How are your judgments and attitudes showing up physically?**
Observe and ask about facial expressions, body movements, posture, gestures, and breathing patterns. Then, ask employees to pay attention to how they are responding physically to their judgments. This will help them recognize the ways in which their judgments are af-

fecting their physical being. It may be tense shoulders, rolling eyes, or something less noticeable, but these physical manifestations of judgments and attitudes can either aid or block success. Again, your employee may not even be aware of their physicality, a great manger helps create awareness and the necessary shifts.

**What actions will your current thinking (judgments, attitude, speech, or physicality) likely inspire?**
The goal of this question is to help employees create needed shifts in their approach to reaching their desired results. Sometimes the slightest adjustment in one area can open up new possibilities. A sustainable shift will occur when people identify the need for it themselves.

> *Allowing them to devise solutions with no constraints can help them create new solutions.*

**If nothing was in your way, and you knew that everything would all turn out well, what would you do?**
The stories that your employees tell themselves may prevent them from reaching their goals. They may perceive obstacles that aren't actually present, or at least not as insurmountable as they first thought. Allowing employees to devise solutions with no restrictions or constraints can help them create new stories and work to attain solutions.

**May I offer you my observations?**
By offering your observations, you can help your employees reassess their judgments and see a situation in a different light. As a coach, you can actually move beyond just facilitating the conversation—you can offer a new lens through which employees can view themselves. Your employee might agree with your observations or completely reject them. Either way, you're helping your employee gain the clarity needed to shift his or her judgments. Unsolicited comments and

observations can trigger a defensive response. Asking if you may offer your observations *before* offering them demonstrates respect for their ability and a willingness to listen, so always ask before offering.

**What new practices can you put into place to ensure your success?**
Developing new practices and habits will help employees reach their goals. Asking employees to formulate their new practices allows them to take ownership of their future and gives you a common connection point. Over time, you can check in on their new practices and help determine if they are working or not. This is a perfect opportunity to offer suggestions and brainstorm new practices as needed.

**Are you willing to take action? By when? And if not, why not?**
Without action, the best of plans are just ideas. If an employee is unwilling to take action, your Powerful Questions must focus on exactly what is holding them back and why. This may require greater understanding about your employee's judgments of the situation at hand. While you may repeat some previously asked questions, you'll be asking within a new context—that of an *unwillingness to take action*.

> *As you create a sense of urgency, you'll inspire accountability and action toward the goal.*

If your employee *is* willing to take action, then proceed. Focus on the first steps, timing, accountability, and establishing future coaching conversations. Actions, behaviors, and results that you discuss, and even agree on, may not happen without accountability. Establishing a timeline can create a sense of urgency and inspire activity toward the goal. A timeline is also an opportunity to check on progress and coach as needed along the way.

**The Bonus Question:  What Else?**

This question can be used at almost any time in a coaching conversation.  Keep this question in mind and incorporate it as needed. When you're coaching, the most important voice belongs to your employee.  Even though you are asking Powerful Questions to help them be their best, you're still their boss, and it can be difficult for them to think of everything they want to say in the moment.  Asking this question can give your employee an opportunity to truly reflect and bring additional thoughts to the surface.  The question must be followed by a pause, just as if it were part of the question.  Say, "What else . . . ?"  *And then stop.*  Allow what could be an awkward silence to exist.  Don't worry—your employee will likely fill that silence with the real issue that's waiting to be unlocked.

It is important that you ask the Powerful Questions in a way that is natural and aligned with your personal style. You can modify the questions as needed to ensure they are relevant to the conversation you are having.  Let's see what an interaction looks like when Powerful Questions are used in a coaching conversation. In this instance we will use many of the specific words outlined in the 12 Powerful Questions. This language may feel or sound foreign at first. Give it time; you, and your employees, will get used to it and it will eventually become a more natural way of communication with each other.

Nigel is a sales manager at a boutique consulting firm. He recently announced a new sales structure that he believes will better help his firm reach its growth targets. Joseph is one of the team's most successful sales consultants and Nigel senses that Joseph is not onboard with the new sales structure.

Nigel visits Joseph in his private office to better understand Joseph's perspective on the newly announced sales structure.

**Nigel:** Hey Joseph, I stopped by to chat about the new sales structure. **Is this a good time to talk?**

**Joseph:** Come on in, I was a just about to send you an email asking if we could talk.

**Nigel:** Sounds like good timing! How about we both take a seat here in front of your desk.

**Joseph:** Sure, let's have a seat.

**Nigel:** Joseph, **what is most important for you to talk about?**

**Joseph:** I'm really ticked about the changes in the sales structure, and I'm wondering what in the world we hope to gain by changing our bonus from team performance to individual performance?

**Nigel:** Let's talk about that, but first, **can you tell me more** about your concerns?

**Joseph:** We've been team selling for years and the new sales and bonus structure is setting everyone up to be solo acts. I know we need to grow sales, and this sure as hell isn't the way to go about it. This new structure could tear our team apart.

**Nigel:** I understand. You see the need to grow sales and you're concerned about the impact the structure may have on the team.

**Joseph:** You got it!

**Nigel: How is that affecting your attitude** about the future?

**Joseph:** What do you mean?

**Nigel:** How are your concerns affecting the way you are looking at your future in this job and with the company?

**Joseph:** I feel unsure. I'm not confident that I'm going to be as effective working independently as I was with the team.

**Nigel:** I want to make sure I'm clear. **Your judgment** is that you were successful in the old structure, and you are worried that you may not do as well in this new one. **Is that correct?**

**Joseph:** That pretty much sums it up. Today I am getting new leads from a junior member of my team and I am converting them into new business. That system works! I can close a deal once I have a lead, but I'm not great at finding them.

**Nigel:** What else?

**Joseph:** I've never had to generate leads before! I can lose income, and I don't want to look like a loser if I can't find new leads.

**Nigel:** Joseph, I want to pause for a moment and take a look at the words you are using to describe your attitude. You say you're **not good** at finding new business leads, you're **afraid** to look like a **loser** and you could **lose income**. **How do you see your language impacting your ability** to achieve the results you want?

**Joseph:** I get your point, I guess my language is kind of negative but I'm not sure how my word choices could impact my results.

**Nigel:** Think about it, and for that matter, think about **what actions your current judgments**, **attitude**, **and speech** will likely inspire.

**Joseph:** Yeah, not very positive actions. Don't get me wrong, I can see how growing sales could actually increase my income, which would be a very good thing. I just need to figure out how to get sales leads for myself.

**Nigel:** So **what is holding you back** from making a plan to find those leads?

**Joseph:** I've been successful under the same sales structure for ten years. I don't really know where to start!

**Nigel:** May I offer you my observations?

**Joseph:** Go ahead.

**Nigel:** Joseph, you are awesome at building relationships, and your clients love you! I think that you can leverage the great relationships you have built to help you find the new leads.

**Joseph:** Yeah, thanks. I'm proud of those relationships. I had visions in my head about sitting at my desk and cold calling all day. Working with my clients to find new leads feels a lot better. I can see myself doing that.

**Nigel:** **If nothing were in your way** and you knew it would all turn out well, **what would you do** to ensure your continued success?

**Joseph:** Well, besides getting referrals from my existing clients, I also could call on dormant accounts.

**Nigel:  What else?**

**Joseph:**  Let me think . . . I could talk to our marketing director about how to increase my inbound leads.

**Nigel:**  I heard you mention three distinct lead-generating activities—referrals, dormant accounts, and encouraging more inbound calls through marketing.

**Joseph:**  Hey, I can also call the potential clients who chose competitors over us in the past.  I'd like to see if I could take another crack at them.

**Nigel:**  Great, so now you have mentioned four things you could do! **What new practices** can you put into place to ensure your success?

**Joseph:**  I can start by scheduling a few hours every day to reach out to existing and dormant and potential clients.

Nigel:  **What else?...**

**Joseph:**  I will also set up a meeting with marketing to talk about inbound leads.

**Nigel:**  Is this a plan you can take **action** on?

**Joseph:**  I think I can make this work, yes.

**Nigel:**  Joseph, **you look a lot less stressed out** compared to when we started to talk.

**Joseph:**  Yeah, yeah, I guess I am. You know, I was really nervous about the changes.  I still am, but I think I have a plan now.

**Nigel:  When do you think you can start** to take action?

**Joseph:**  I'll block the time on my calendar today and will hit the phones first thing tomorrow.

**Nigel:**  If you don't mind, **let's talk again** in a few weeks to see how your plan is working out.

**Joseph:**  Thanks, in a while I'll send you a calendar invite.


## They're Portable!

You can take these simple yet effective Powerful Questions wherever you go.  Regardless of the subject, these questions will help your employees think and say more.  Through reflective thinking, and by digging beneath the surface of initial thoughts and emotions, your employees can and will come to their own conclusions about how to support their own success and that of their teams and the company. And, as a Great Manager, you will help guide your employees to achieve this success when they might otherwise have been unable or unequipped to do so.

> *Coaching conversations will help translate strategy and expectations into consistently well-executed actions.*

When these Powerful Questions, or variations of them, are used effectively, they can spark a true coaching conversation. A coaching conversation doesn't need to be introduced or explained as such. However, it requires you, as a Great Manager, to ask Powerful Questions and listen actively. You need to offer observations and facilitate shifts in beliefs, actions, and behaviors. Then, listen and share your observations again.

Remember, not every conversation needs to be, or should be, a coaching conversation. Some conversations require you to tell employees important information, including organizational and team strategies, individual results, and the team scorecard. When setting clear expectations, telling is more effective and direct than asking. But coaching conversations may be appropriate for translating strategy and expectations into consistently well-executed actions that produce desired results.

A successful coaching conversation also requires you to take a genuine interest in your employees. You can't fake this. It's not something you can learn in a book. If you're not interested in the growth and development of others, give this book to someone who is and consider a role as an individual contributor. If your care for the development of others is authentic, and you truly want to be a Great Manager, keep reading.

The ability to have coaching conversations is a skill you can master. In the chapters ahead, you will learn about the JASPAR coaching model that will help you build your skills. Of course, just following a process or reciting Powerful Questions doesn't constitute a coaching conversation. You will be the defining element that will determine whether you're a great coach, and therefore, a Great Manager.

## Worksheet for Chapter 3
## The 12 Powerful Questions

1.  As you reflect on the Powerful Questions in this chapter and the bonus question, which ones are you most eager to put into practice with your employees?

2.  What benefits to your employees and the business do you foresee by using Powerful Questions?

3.  Which questions are you most skeptical about putting into practice, and why?

4. Consider your specific company and team. Write three or more of your own Powerful Questions and verify that they are indeed Powerful by using this grid. Remember, to be a Powerful Question, all four of the boxes must be checked

| Question | Is the question open-ended? | Is the question non-judgmental? | Is the question provocative? | Is the question respectful? | RESULT: Is this a Powerful Question? |
|---|---|---|---|---|---|
| | | | | | |
| | | | | | |
| | | | | | |

5. Think about an upcoming conversation that you want to have with one of your employees. List the Powerful Questions that will guide the discussion and promote the best possible outcome.

# Chapter 4

## Trust - A Must for Coaching Conversations

A Great Manager uses coaching conversations to shine a light on results that their employees are focused on achieving. These conversations allow employees to discover the shifts they need to make to create those results. Through ongoing coaching conversations, you'll help your employees significantly improve their level of engagement in the business and the results they deliver.

Coaching an individual is most successful when the employee has an established *bond of trust* with you, is *motivated to succeed*, and *commits to regular, ongoing coaching conversations.*

When any of these elements is missing, the coaching conversation is less likely to be successful, beneficial, or to create real shifts. When all the elements are in place, however, individual coaching is a powerful tool that can help employees perform and contribute at their highest level—and with the greatest satisfaction.

Trust is possibly the most important of these three elements. I advise not entering into a coaching conversation until you have established at least the *beginning* of a relationship of trust. As a coach, you'll be asking your employees for real examples and stories about their experiences, and you'll share stories of your own. Without the foundation of a trusting relationship, you each may have difficulty sharing those stories openly. In a new relationship with an employee, a Great Manager takes the first steps in building trust by demonstrating openness and vulnerability *first*. Once the relationship has been established, you can demonstrate credibility, commitment, and confidence by scheduling regular coaching conversations.

Coaching individual employees can be done both informally and formally. For informal coaching, the conversation might be impromptu and address a routine work situation. Formal coaching conversations are planned, and they may address performance-related issues or other significant topics. In either case, as a Great Manager, be sure that the conversation is confidential and is held in a private setting at a time when the employee can participate fully. Individual employee coaching conversations work well for addressing everyday work issues and performance issues, as well as for organizational and individual transformation, development of high-potential talent, or helping low performers improve or move to a role (or company) that better suits them.

Here's everything you need to get started with coaching conversations:

- **Explain the concept of coaching conversations.** If this is a new approach for you or if you are new to your employees, start with an introduction of the technique. Some people hear "coaching" and think "punishment." They may think coaching is about deficiencies or problems. Others may think it means getting advice or instructions. And some will think it's some corporate mumbo-jumbo intended to make them feel warm and fuzzy. Make it clear that coaching is a partnership between you and your employees, and that any topic can be discussed with the intention of helping achieve results for the employee, the team and for the company. Assure the employee that this dialogue is about *them*, and that you won't discuss other employees or compare performance.

- **Clarify the roles and set ground rules.** Explain that your role as a coach is to ask questions, listen, and offer observations. Ask them to be honest and open to making shifts in their beliefs and behaviors that will help achieve the results you want. Also, you need ground rules. Start with these areas and add your own: No distractions (cell phones, etc.—off). Privacy—a quiet place. A certain length—decided in advance. Confidentiality—to ensure trust. Openness—believing that both parties have positive intentions. Build these to fit your situation accordingly.

- **Be comfortable.** Don't coach when you're tired, angry, frustrated, or emotional. If you're not in your best frame of mind, delay your coaching conversation rather than taking the risk that it might go poorly. Also, the way you are seated physically can impact your coaching conversation interaction. Sitting across from the employee or at your desk looks and feels adversarial, and may create expectations that you're going to tell them the answers or give them advice. Try sitting at a right angle from your employee when coaching one-on-one, making sure you are in chairs of the same height. This type of arrangement promotes informality and a feeling of partnership.

- **Establish the coaching topic.** Remember, what's important to your employee to talk about must be important to you, too. Regardless of who initiated the conversation, identify what is most meaningful to talk about, work on, or resolve. Encourage your employee to get clearer and crisper throughout the conversation. Ask them to express their story, and then distill it into a sentence or a bullet point. This process will create focus and help your employee become clear about what is important to them, which in turn, will foster easier understanding of the changes that may be needed.

- **Be yourself.** Throughout the conversation, maintain your flexibility and open-mindedness, and be agile enough to take the conversation where it needs to go. But most important, *be yourself*. Don't rehearse or create a script. You don't want to show up with an agenda that has to be completed. Being authentic, honest, and open with your employees can strengthen your relationships, positively impacting the outcomes of coaching conversations. When you admit that you don't know the next step or you highlight mistakes you've made and learned from, you allow your employees to make mistakes, knowing they have your support.

- **Ask Powerful Questions and listen actively.** Once the topic of the conversation is established, ask Powerful Questions and let the employee talk. This will put them at ease and help you gain greater insight. Offer your observations only after you have encouraged your employee to completely exhaust their thoughts.

- **Don't give them the answers.** Sometimes an employee or your team will ask for answers—"Just tell me what you want me to do!" As tempting as this may seem, *don't do it!* Most times, employees need just a bit of help in discovering the answers for themselves, and you can help them achieve that through coaching conversations. Facilitating a brainstorming activity—such as asking them to list everything that comes to mind about a problem or potential solution—can spark a dialogue that leads employees to their own solutions. When employees discover their own solutions with your coaching assistance, they yield far greater results than when simply told what to do, or dictated a course of action to follow.

- **Offer observations.** Asking permission before offering observations is important. Always preface your suggestions with, "May I share my observations?" or "Are you open to hearing my observations?" The answer will help you gauge your employee's receptiveness and readiness for input. Providing observations (rather than giving answers) avoids creating dependency and won't undermine your employees' ability to solve things for themselves. If you perceive that your employee isn't receptive during this particular coaching conversation, save your observations for another time. And don't take this as a sign of failure on your part. The employee may simply need time to process the conversation before continuing. If your employee wants your observations, describe the specific behaviors you notice and ask for their thoughts.

- **Wrap it up neatly and ask for feedback.** Before ending any coaching conversation, ask your employee to identify two or three insights they learned. Ask what they plan to do based on those insights and what they think might happen. The employee's responses may very well form the basis for your next coaching conversation. Then, ask for feedback. You may find that you need to modify your style. Be receptive and take the feedback as a gift. Great Managers are always learning and modeling best practices—even the skill of receiving feedback.

**Let's see how this manager tees up a coaching conversation:**
Angela is a hard-working, tenured director at a manufacturing plant. She considers herself a no-nonsense "get 'er done" type. Her organization is going through a process reengineering initiative and she

plays a key role on the team responsible for designing and implementing the new process.

Angela has been working as part of the process reengineering team for several months and her manager, Margie, wants to discuss Angela's progress and offer her some of her observations. Margie calls Angela to set up a time to meet.

**Margie:** If you are available for lunch today, can we meet at the corner café at noon?
**Angela:** Sure, is this a working lunch? Do I need to bring anything?
**Margie:** Just bring yourself. I'd like to have a coaching conversation with you about the process reengineering initiative.
**Angela:** Uh oh! A "coaching conversation." That doesn't sound good at all!
**Margie:** Let me explain. Coaching conversation is just another way of saying that I would like to establish more of a partnership where we can discuss any topic to make sure we're achieving the results that you want and that the business needs. Through a coaching conversation, we can discuss various aspects of work and performance—not only when something is wrong.
**Angela:** OK, you can tell me more at the café; I need to grab my other line.
**Margie:** See you at noon.

Once Angela and Margie have settled in at their lunch table they resume their conversation.

**Angela:** Margie, tell me more about what you mean by a coaching conversation.
**Margie:** Well, as a manager I am trying to get better at coaching the team and everyone on it. By coaching, I mean I am going to be asking more questions, listening, and offering my observations. And

your role is to be honest and open to making shifts where needed so you and the company can get the results we all want. How does that sound?

**Angela:** Sounds better than when you first said coaching! I thought I might be in trouble.

**Margie:** Well, I'm glad we cleared that up. There are a few ground rules that we should set up. Let's both keep our cell phones off, and when we have a coaching conversation, it will always be in a private place like this. Let's also agree that anything said in a coaching conversation will be confidential. And we'll set a time limit. For today, I think we will need about fifteen minutes? Does that work for you?

**Angela:** My cell phone is silenced; let's get started. I have to warn you, we are going to have to talk with our mouths full and you better tell me if I have lettuce in my teeth!

**Margie:** There are a few things I wanted to make sure we cover about the process reengineering initiative, but first, I want to know what is most important for you to talk about.

**Angela:** I don't know. Since you had a few things you wanted to cover, why don't you go first?

**Margie:** Okay. I'm curious, what are you trying to achieve in the process reengineering initiative? What results are you aiming for?

**Angela:** I want to do a good job in my portion of the process—I am shooting for accuracy, effectiveness, and timeliness.

**Margie:** What kind of results are you getting now?

**Angela:** I'm not making the type of progress I was hoping for.

**Margie:** Can you say more?

**Angela:** I hate to admit it, but I have missed several deadlines.

**Margie:** What else?

**Angela:** Well, my accuracy is off, but that's because I can't get my work done because of all these stupid meetings about the project. It's ridiculous! We spend more time together talking about the project than actually working on it. The project meetings are waste of time!

**Margie:** Angela, "waste of time" sounds like your opinion. Instead, tell me what's *really* happening. You know—the facts, and then tell me about the emotions you're adding to the story.

**Angela:** Oh, that's just me venting. I am really frustrated!

**Margie:** Venting is fine. Now, let's get into what parts of your comments were venting and what were the facts?

**Angela:** The facts are that we meet two or three times a week as a team. My venting was about those meetings being ridiculous and a waste of time.

**Margie:** What I have heard so far is that your accuracy and ability to meet deadlines are not up to snuff and that you find the project meetings to be a waste of time. I also heard you say you want to deliver excellence in your part of the project. How'd I do?

**Angela:** You summed that up pretty well. That covers it. I tell you, I'd be more efficient if I could just be left alone to do what I need to do.

**Margie:** May I share an observation?

**Angela:** Sure, go ahead.

**Margie:** I see some reluctance on your part to partner with others on this initiative.

**Angela:** Why would you say that? I think I'm a pretty good collaborator.

**Margie:** Well, some of the words that you used are "stupid," "ridiculous," and "a waste of time." If you're showing up to meetings where collaboration is required and you're thinking they are stupid and a waste of time, are you going to be able to be a great collaborator?

**Angela:** Ugh, I don't know. I guess not. I just want to do my work!

**Margie:** Angela, take a minute and think about how frustrated you are. Has your frustration shown up in you physically?

**Angela:** Yes! The thought of going into another one of those meetings makes me tense up from head to toe—that's how much it bothers me to have to sit there.

**Margie:** Let's put this story together. You walk into the process re-engineering meetings thinking they are stupid and a waste of time and your body is tensed up from head to toe. Do you think that these things might be noticeable to others?

**Angela:** That's interesting. I haven't much thought about it, but I suppose it could.

**Margie:** What actions will your current story or thinking likely inspire?

**Angela:** Well, I am not getting the results I want, so . . . maybe that says it all.

**Margie:** What do you think is the real purpose of those meetings?

**Angela:** I'm sure they're meant to help everyone know what's going on with the project. But not everyone needs to know everything, do they?

**Margie:** You tell me. What are the benefits of knowing what others are working on?

**Angela:** Benefits? I know there is a benefit in seeing how the pieces fit together, but I think we can do that at the end of the project.

**Margie:** How can you think about that differently?

**Angela:** What do you mean?

**Margie:** Well, try turning your comment about "fitting the pieces together at the end" around. What are the benefits of seeing how the pieces fit together in the beginning of the process—and the middle, for that matter?

**Angela:** I see. Let me think for a minute. Okay, the meetings may help us avoid any big slip-ups or surprises at the end.

**Margie:** Okay, Angela, now look at the meetings from that perspective. Are they still a big waste of time?

**Angela:** Yeah, not so much.

**Margie:** Angela, your results aren't what you expect from yourself, and your experience with the team hasn't been a great one. If nothing were in your way and you knew it would all turn out well, what would you do to change that?

**Angela:** In a perfect world, I'd bring the problems I'm having with my part of the process to the meetings and ask for help.

**Margie:** Sounds good to me! What's holding you back from doing that?

**Angela:** It's embarrassing! I didn't want to seem incompetent.

**Margie:** Are you incompetent?

**Angela:** No, I'm *not* incompetent! I just don't want to look foolish.

**Margie:** So what do you want to do about it? What new practices can you put in place that won't make you look foolish but will help you get the results you want?

**Angela:** I could bring the accuracy issue up at the next team meeting; I haven't been able to figure that out on my own.

**Margie:** That sounds like a great start. Are you willing to do it?

**Angela:** I'll give it a try. I'll get accuracy added to the next agenda.

**Margie:** So what did you think of our coaching conversation?

**Angela:** Well, you did help me to look at the situation differently, and I appreciate that.

**Margie:** Should we split the chocolate cake for dessert?

**Angela:** One dessert, two forks, and you can get the check!

And that's it! As a Great Manager, there are countless topics on which to coach your employees. Remember, coaching doesn't happen only in a formal or scheduled conversation, it can occur wherever and whenever an employee's privacy can be respected. Also keep in mind that each person will respond differently to this approach.

Above all, don't worry about being the perfect coach or flawlessly following each step. Your employees asking for more coaching conversations is the true mark of success.

### Time to Get Your Feet Wet

The ASK coaching model is simple and effective. At this point you already have the basic tools to begin effectively coaching your employees to achieve desired results. By asking 12 Powerful Questions and building relationships of trust with your employees you can, armed only with what you have learned to this point, begin reaping the rewards of the ASK coaching model.

There's no need to wait—jump right in and begin! You will be surprised to see how quickly using the ASK coaching model and 12 Powerful Questions will garner positive results. If you put this book down right now and simply apply what you've learned so far, you will already be managing at a higher level than most, and I encourage you to start using what you've learned right away.

However, for those who wish to take things further and become truly Great Managers, there is even more to learn. We have covered the core philosophy of coaching as a management tool, 12 Powerful Questions that align you and your employee on important topics to discuss in order to understand your employee's perspectives and kickstart shifts in action. Now, for those who wish to become even more effective, it's time to delve more deeply into how to apply Powerful Questions to six specific areas in the JASPAR framework that will support your coaching efforts. The JASPAR framework will help you and your employees gain deeper insight and understanding into the judgments, attitudes, speech, and physicality that lead to the actions, and results that either inhibit, or drive success in the workplace. It represents an opportunity for you as a Great Manager, and for those you manage, to reach new heights of success. Like all journeys into the unknown, it will be both exciting and nerve-wracking, and will leave all participants with a broader perspective and a new, positive view of what is possible. When you are ready to take the next step, read on!

## Worksheet for Chapter 4
## Trust - A Must for Coaching Conversations

1.  In the coaching conversation in this chapter, the coach had a specific performance issue to discuss with her employee. Plan a coaching conversation that you'd like to have with your employee or team, keeping in mind:

    *   Individual styles and strengths

    *   Specific opportunities to bring to your employee

    *   Questions to ensure that what's important to them is brought out in the conversation

2.  What Powerful Questions will you ask? Keep in mind that you may need to change or modify these as you go, depending on your employee's response and any unexpected direction the conversation may take.

# Chapter 5

## The JASPAR Coaching Model

# Meet JASPAR!

Whenever I see the words "Assembly Required," I cringe. When my kids were small and I needed to put together a new bike, the first thing I'd do was throw away the instructions. And often, when the bike was finished, there were leftover parts on the floor. I'd wonder what I'd done wrong and cross my fingers that the bike was really safe for my kid to ride.

Instructions can seem overwhelming and confusing. But when we follow them correctly, they also lead us to the results we want. This is true in coaching conversations as well. Now, nobody wants to read instructions on how to have a conversation. That should be something we can figure out on our own—like assembling a bike, right? Seems easy enough. Ah, but conversations are more complicated when you're leading individuals or teams toward business results. There are steps, like instructions, that Great Managers take when they have coaching conversations.

My intention is to give you very simple instructions that will help you bring out the best in your teams through coaching conversations. When you follow these instructions, you won't have extra parts (or bruised employees) lying on the floor.

In this chapter, you'll be introduced to the JASPAR coaching framework and learn to use Powerful Questions in six phases:

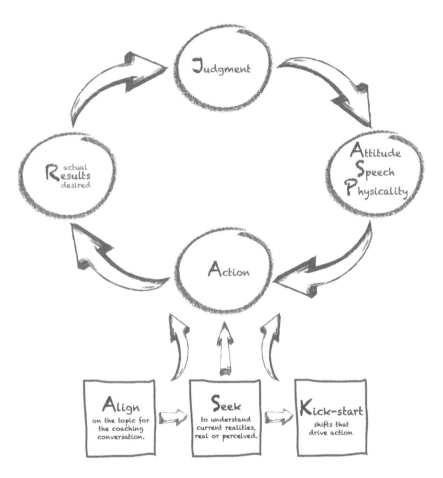

**Uncovering JUDGMENTS, assessments, or opinions**: identifying the judgments or opinions held by your employees can help both of you better understand how they view a particular situation.

**Identifying ATTITUDES based on Judgments**: your employee's attitude or outlook has a major impact on how they perform their work, how they're viewed by others, and ultimately, on their results.

**Observing language or what we are referring to as SPEECH to see how it supports or blocks your employees from reaching their goals**: speech, or language, and tone of voice can either reinforce negative and defeatist attitudes or support positive ones.

**Noticing your employees' PHYSICALITY**: gestures, movements, and mannerisms communicate what words do not. The manner in which your employees present and carry themselves can tell a story that outweighs words and provides insight to their mindset.

**Establishing ACTIONS that have taken place or need to take place to reach desired results**: the activities that your employees undertake lead to the outcomes they deliver and directly affect their performance and that of the team and company.

**Evaluating RESULTS, consequences, effects, or conclusions**: through their judgments, attitudes, speech, physicality, and actions, your employees produce results. Understanding their *actual* results as opposed to *desired* results is paramount to any employee's success.

As coaches, we listen actively, observe, ask Powerful Questions, and offer our observations. In this way, we help our employees to shift their Judgments, Attitudes, Speech, and Physicality to bring about new or different Actions and Results.

## A Conversation without JASPAR

Let's look at a scenario involving an employee and his manager. We'll first view it from the point of view of a traditional manager, and then we'll apply the JASPAR coaching model that a Great Manager would use.

Michael, a product innovation manager, has been with his company for three years. He's a solid performer, consistently meeting or exceeding his goals in bringing successful new products to market. When a sister division of his organization needs a senior product innovation manager, he is offered the promotion. Michael welcomes the advancement and the additional compensation, even though he considers his new manager, Isabel, to be not all that smart based on his previous exposure to her. When Isabel spoke at the company's annual conference last year, Michael judged her to be far less on the ball than the leader of his current division. He also perceived that the clients he'd be working with would be much larger and, therefore, would demand much lower pricing.

As Michael begins his transition into the sister division, he feels stress every day. His back, shoulders, and neck are almost rigid, and his speech and thoughts follow suit. He tells himself, "My new manager can't help me create a strategy for the development of cost-competitive products. She doesn't know enough! Given the size of my new accounts, I'll have to design very inexpensive offerings and become known as the cheapest provider. Oh, great!"

Isabel and Michael meet just before his first day in his new role to review the marketplace and client needs. Isabel is happy to have someone already experienced in product innovation on her team. Privately, she's thankful that Michael won't need much attention from her, as she's already overloaded with other responsibilities. She tells Michael, "If you need me, shoot me an email, but I know you'll be fine," and wishes him good luck.

At the end of the first quarter, Michael is troubled by his results. The customer satisfaction ratings and sales numbers on the products he's introduced are far below goal. During the first quarter, Isabel contacts him several times and tells him what she would do in his place.

At Michael's three-month review, Isabel tells Michael that he hasn't performed well. She reminds him that he didn't take her advice during their previous conversations. Finally, she tells Michael that several of his clients have complained that he's inflexible and isn't providing the level of consultation they expected.

Isabel is losing confidence in Michael, and she gets anxious thinking about yet another difficult conversation. She tells herself, "We made a mistake by promoting Michael to a senior manager after only three years. He's not ready for this role. He'll never last!" At the same time, Michael is angry about the feedback, and he's determined to prove his manager wrong. He again commits himself to work based on his judgments.

By the end of the second quarter, Michael's results are even worse. He quits his job, saying that his manager wasn't knowledgeable and his company wasn't price-competitive in the territory.

In essence, Isabel and Michael both created an outcome based on their judgments. Were they (also) based on fact? Their judgments, attitudes, speech, and even Michael's physicality, ultimately influenced the actions they undertook and the results they obtained.

If Isabel were acting as a Great Manager, she would have known how to coach Michael in order to achieve the results that they both wanted.

Isabel failed to engage Michael and to make coaching a priority. Without knowing more about how Michael had judged the division he was joining, the customers, and the competition, Isabel couldn't possibly have known the beliefs he had already established.

## A Better Conversation

Let's see how a different result could have been achieved if Isabel had used the JASPAR coaching framework.

Isabel and Michael have scheduled a time to meet via video conference to discuss Michael's new role:

**Isabel:** Hi Michael, can you hear and see me okay?
**Michael:** Loud and clear, Isabel.
**Isabel:** Fantastic! I'm sorry we weren't able to meet in person. Does this time still work for you to talk?
**Michael:** Sure, Isabel, this time still works. I've been looking forward to it.
**Isabel:** So have I. Before we get started, I want you to know how much I value the experience and tenure you bring.
**Michael:** Thanks. You know, I'm hoping I can do as well here as I did in my last position. It's a little nerve wracking to leave a great gig when you're at the top of your game and jump into the unknown.
**Isabel:** Michael, I am sure you're going to do really well here, and I want to make sure I know what your goals are so I know how to best support you. Have you given any thought to what you want to accomplish in your new role?

**Michael:** In my last job, I built really strong relationships with my customers, so I know I want to do the same with my new customers. I want to give my customers what they need and want, and I want to blow away my quota at the same time.

**Isabel:** What else?

**Michael:** Well, I don't want to sound greedy, but I want to hit my bonus—I've hit full bonus for the past three years! I want to develop successful products for our customers, make money for the company, and hit bonus—I want it all!

**Isabel:** Let me make sure I understand; your motivation comes from company growth, customer satisfaction, and your continued success.

**Michael:** Yes, that's it. I call it the business trifecta.

**Isabel:** That's funny; it is the business trifecta, isn't it? I'm interested in what your judgments are about your new role.

**Michael:** My judgments? Hmm. Well, I believe that it's similar to the role I've had for the past three years. The biggest difference I see is the size of the accounts and that I will be working with a more senior-level decision maker.

**Isabel:** What excites you about that?

**Michael:** Oh, I think this could be a real growth opportunity. This should give me a chance to deliver much bigger contracts to the company.

**Isabel:** Any concerns about the new position?

**Michael:** I know that these larger accounts in this territory are price sensitive. I'm really going to have to establish myself as the cheapest provider in order to get their business.

**Isabel:** What do you base that judgment on?

**Michael:** Well, that's what I heard from some others in the division, and I have to admit that that is the only thing that stresses me out about the position.

**Isabel:** We don't want you starting a new job all stressed out. Say more about the stress.

**Michael**: It's really no big deal, but when I am really stressed, I have trouble sleeping. Look, I'm starting a new job with new customers and that is bound to stress anyone out.

**Isabel**: Well, we certainly want you at your best, and I don't think that's possible if you aren't sleeping well! Let's see if we can get you more comfortable. What can you do to check the facts about your new customers and see if they really are price buyers or not?

**Michael**: Well, I know what I've heard, but I guess I could talk to Bill. He's the senior sales executive; he should know.

**Isabel**: What else?

**Michael**: I could look at past invoices and look at the buying history for my new accounts, which will really give me some solid information.

**Isabel**: Is there anyone else who can help you better understand the market?

**Michael**: Yeah, I could talk with our actual customers, but I'm not sure how I can get them to tell me whether they're price buyers or not.

**Isabel**: What have you done in the past to get to know your customers better?

**Michael**: That's simple—I just asked my customers what's important to them!

**Isabel**: Is that something you are willing to try with your new customers?

**Michael**: Sure, it's simple enough and would also be a great way to start to build these new relationships.

**Isabel**: You mentioned talking to Bill, reviewing past invoices, and asking your new customers what's important to them. Are those ideas you can take action on?

**Michael**: For sure. I can do all of these things, no problem.

**Isabel**: I'll bet once you start to take the actions we've reviewed, you'll start sleeping a lot better.

**Michael**: I hope so. I'll take a walk down to accounts receivable and ask for copies of invoices, and I'll set up lunch with Bill. I think you're in the office next week, can we get back together then so I can tell you what I find?

**Isabel**: That sounds like a plan! Is there anything else important for us to discuss today?

**Michael**: No, I think we covered it all. Thank you, it was a good conversation.

**Isabel**: Thank you. I think you're going to be very successful here; I'll see you next week in the office, and I can't wait to hear what you find out!

If we were to fast forward three months and listen in on Michael's first quarterly review with Isabel, we would find him relaxed, confident, and engaged in one of their many conversations about the marketplace, clients, and his performance. Michael and Isabel have built a solid working relationship, and Michael is doing very well.

### Better Than a Bicycle

Anyone can follow these instructions for a coaching conversation. This method might seem simple, almost intuitive—because it is! Yet, it may not seem natural because it isn't the way managing has been modeled for us. As a Great Manager, you'll need to let go of some old ways of interacting with employees and adopt new skills and techniques. You'll also have to prepare your employees, explaining what a real coaching conversation is and what they can expect from you.

Conversations like these are personal and interactive and may initially seem challenging (just like reading instructions). But once you start having them, you'll be rewarded with better communications with employees, resulting in a more collaborative work environment and improved business results.

A well-assembled bike is more than just a toy. It supports your child safely and takes him where he wants to go. It opens up new possibilities; it gives him independence he's never had before and sparks an eagerness to explore new things on his own.

This JASPAR framework allows you to do the same thing for your employees.

## Worksheet for Chapter 5
## The JASPAR Coaching Model

1. Now that you've been introduced to JASPAR, what are your judgments so far? What attitude or outlook do you have based on these judgments?

2. Review the original story of Michael and Isabel. What words describe Michael and Isabel's judgments, attitudes, speech, physicality, actions, and results?

| **Michael** | **Isabel** |
| --- | --- |
| Judgment | Judgment |
| Attitude | Attitude |
| Speech | Speech |
| Physicality | Physicality |

Actions

Actions

Results

Results

3. As you observed a better way for Michael and Isabel to communicate, what stood out to you as most powerful about their conversation? What did you learn from this example that you can use in your own conversations?

4. What old ways of interacting with your employees might you need to let go of?

5. As you think about preparing and educating your employees about what a coaching conversation is and what they can expect from you, what is most important for them to know? Document your thoughts as a way to prepare for this conversation about coaching.

# Chapter 6

## "Everyone's Entitled to My Opinion" -

## JUDGMENT

I grew up in my family's business in the garment industry in New Jersey. My dad manufactured and retailed uniforms. He was almost always in the shop or on the retail floor. For a very short period of time, he had a desk, at which he sat rarely. At the edge of that desk stood a little statue of a man with his thumbs pointing to his chest, and the caption at the base of the statue read: Everybody is entitled to their own opinion, as long as it's mine.

Even as a kid, I saw the humor in this. But, in fact, my father, like many managers, led his team based largely on his own opinions or judgments, without necessarily considering those of his employees. All of our employees have judgments, and Great Managers have the ability to uncover these judgments and help shape them to support the goals of the employee, team and company.

## Where Do Judgments Come From?

Like fingerprints, judgments are unique and individual, and they're influenced by our own experiences. Even if they're not based on fact, they're strong enough to affect our attitudes and actions.

Sometimes, judgments are passed from generation to generation. Growing up in my family's business, I was exposed to an entrepreneurial environment. I was the third generation working in the same industry, and my judgment was that working for yourself was the only valuable and meaningful work that you could do. My judgment was that all people who worked for someone else had a less-than-fulfilling work experience, and given the opportunity, they too would be self-employed. It's no surprise that when it was time for me to enter the workforce, I opened my own business and never even considered working for anyone else. My judgment, which I held as a fact, was that being self-employed was the only option.

Judgments can be carried over from one job to another: "All companies are the same. Leaders sit up in their ivory tower with no clue about how the real work gets done on the front line!" No matter what the source, Judgments can entrench people in a mindset that isn't productive, but a Great Manager can coach them into productivity.

## Just Do It My Way

Managers may tell employees what they do wrong, and to "do it this way, not that way." While they may correct or at least change the actions, these managers fail to understand the judgments that cause those actions, so they miss the chance to truly coach their people. As a result, those employees are likely to make subsequent decisions based on those unchanged judgments.

When faulty judgments become our reality, we view things through a specific lens. Great Managers understand that the way *they* see the world may be different from what their *employees* see. They make it part of their job to look through the lenses of their employees as well as their own.

When 15th-century sailors shifted their reality from "the world is flat" to "the world is round," an entirely new set of possibilities became available. And so it is with your employees. By helping to shift employees' judgments, and thus their reality, we can help them see through a new lens and make decisions differently.

> *When 15th-century sailors shifted their reality from "the world is flat" to "the world is round," an entirely new set of possibilities became available.*

Coaching employees to see—and potentially shift—their judgments eliminates the need to tell people what to do and accelerates results. Great Managers uncover the reasons why a particular decision was made or action was taken. When the judgments behind the actions become clear, people can develop new points of view and take new actions based on new awareness.

## Changing a Mindset in a Minute

Great Managers ask Powerful Questions that quickly, effectively, and respectfully highlight their employees' judgments. As the next conversation unfolds, pay close attention to the Powerful Questions used to uncover the judgments and bring new realities and possibilities into view. The questions and conversation style may seem unfamiliar and even uncomfortable at first. It's up to you to tell your employees that you're working on building your coaching capabilities and that you'd like them to be open to a new kind of conversation.

Jason and Tricia have worked together for years. Tricia leads a key department and has recently started to report to Jason. Jason is eager to see how he can support Tricia in leading her team to meet the changing needs of their business and their customers.

During a brief conversation, it became apparent to Jason that Tricia had formed some strong judgments that were keeping her and her team from accomplishing their goals. Given their new working relationship, Jason was anxious to help Tricia and asked her to meet so they could start to address some of the concerns she had mentioned.

Jason suggested that they take a walk together outside instead of meeting in a windowless meeting room. When they met in the lobby of their building, they agreed they would walk from their office to a local park and back—the trip would take them about 40 minutes, which they thought would be enough time to have a meaningful conversation.

**Jason:** Tricia, we have been working at the same company for so many years and now we actually get a chance to work together. I'm excited about it and I'm a little nervous about our new reporting relationship.

**Tricia:** Nervous? Come on, I'm glad I am reporting to you now; I know that you'll have my back.

**Jason:** Well that's a relief. I know it will be fine once we get into a groove. I'm curious, **what's most important for you to talk about** as we kick off our new relationship?

**Tricia:** As I mentioned to you the other day in the office, the demands on my people and my department are out of control! Something needs to be done about the way our people are taking advantage of my team!

**Jason:** Wow, this seems like a real hot button for you. **Can you give me a specific example** to help me understand?

**Tricia:** Well, last Tuesday, Jordan called at 4:00 p.m. with a project that needed to be done by 9:00 on Wednesday morning! That meant that one of my people had to stay until 7:00 to finish it while Jordan struts his butt out the door at 5:00 on the nose. He could have damn well handed off that project long before 4:00 p.m. He *knew* it would take more than an hour, but he just doesn't care if someone has to work late as long as that someone isn't him. The least he could have done was to let us know about this project as soon as he found out about it.

**Jason:** Tricia, let's talk about what's really happening. Say some more about what the facts of the story are, and then we can talk about **what judgments you added to your story.**

**Tricia:** I don't understand—what do you mean?

**Jason:** A *judgment* is your opinion or conclusion. It's how you view a situation. A *fact* is something that you can verify, like the times that you mentioned.

**Tricia:** Ok, ok, I get it. Let me start with my judgment, that's easier. My judgment is that my team is being taken advantage of! We get unrealistic deadlines and nobody respects our processes or our personal time.

**Jason:** So, based on your judgments, **what attitude do you have?**

**Tricia:** Attitude? A bad one! I'm mad, and this isn't fair!

**Manager:** I heard you say that Jordan could have given you this project long before 4:00, and that he knew how long it would take. **Is that your judgment, or is that a fact?**

**Tricia:** Oh come on! He's been working here for years!

**Manager:** Tricia, I'm sorry, but that doesn't answer the question.

**Tricia:** OK (sigh). According to your definition, those are my *judgments*.

**Jason:** Let's just assume that Jordan had positive intentions—that he didn't intentionally mean to wreck your day. **What other conclusion could you reach?**

**Tricia:** I guess it's possible that Jordan's client could have sprung the request on him at the last minute.

**Manager: What else?**

**Tricia:** Well, I suppose it's possible that Jordan doesn't know how long it takes us to do our work.

**Jason:** All right, it sounds to me like the problems we need to solve are that your team is faced with short timelines and very little notice. Is that right?

**Tricia:** Wow, you boiled down everything I just said into those two little things. Yeah, it sounds like it does come down to that.

**Jason:** Good, I'm glad we're clear. So, ideally, what would you like to see happen? **What are your desired results?**

**Tricia:** I want 24 hours' notice on any project deadline. This issue of the deadline is coming up more and more often.

**Jason:** Why do you think that is?

**Tricia:** Well, I've been thinking that our people don't care about how they impact my team, but as I think about it, our business is growing really fast and our customers are getting more and more demanding.

**Jason:** Ah! I'm noticing a shift in your thinking. Say more about your expectations about 24 hours' notice. Given what you just said about the changes in the business, **would you say that's realistic**?

**Tricia:** Well, given how we're growing these days, it may *not* be totally realistic.

**Jason: How might you look at this differently?**

**Tricia:** Hmmm, um . . . a couple of things come to mind. We could hire some flexible resources; you know, contract employees to handle some of the shorter timelines.

**Jason:** What else?

**Tricia:** I might offer some internal training about our process to help people understand the impact that advance notice has on our schedules *and* quality of work.

**Jason:** Tricia, we're almost back to the office and I want to make sure we finish our conversation before we walk back in the building. Based on our talk, **how have your judgments changed**?

**Tricia:** Ha, surprisingly enough I think my team needs to make some changes. Don't get me wrong, others need to change, too, but I do see things differently. It's a two-way street, and I'm going to need your help.

**Jason:** For sure! It looks like we have a great project to dig into together.

This conversation helped Tricia to identify the judgments that were standing in her way. As a result, she was able to consider the changing needs of customers, and identify how she and her team might need to adjust.

It's tempting to just tell your employee what you think. Many managers have been trained or are just naturally inclined to say something like this: "Tricia, you don't understand! There are a whole bunch of things that could cause timelines to be shorter. People aren't giving you short notice just to drive you crazy. Don't just blame the people —go find out what's really going on!"

While that approach saves time—and it's often the way that managers act when faced with daily business pressures—it's much less effective than a two-way coaching dialogue. Powerful Questions allow employees to view their actions in a clear light, think about different perspectives, and even see their own judgments as just that—*their judgments*. Most importantly, Powerful Questions create possibilities that will positively impact their attitude, speech, how they carry themselves physically, their future actions, and the end results.

Everyone is indeed entitled to their own opinions, and as a Great Manager, you get to uncover what they are. Here are some additional Powerful Questions that can be used to uncover judgments and bring new realities and possibilities into view:

- What are your perceptions?
- How would you judge that?
- What beliefs do you hold?
- What thoughts are you basing your actions on?

- Is what you are saying a fact or your opinion?
- Can you separate your judgments from the facts?
- What events have helped to form your point of view?
- Can you talk about specific examples so I can better understand?
- What led you to that conclusion?
- What makes you say that?
- What other possibilities have you considered?
- How might you look at that differently?
- What other conclusions could you reach?
- When you reconsider your judgments and the facts, what new insights are now available?
- Based on what you know now, how has your judgment changed?
- If you were in the position of the other person, what might you see?
- If you assumed the other person's intent was positive, how would that change your outlook?
- Has your assessment changed?

## Worksheet for Chapter 6
## "Everyone's Entitled to My Opinion" -
## JUDGMENT

1. Think back to the example of the 15th-century sailors and how they had to shift their reality from "the world is flat" to "the world is round." What major shifts have *you* made in *your* thinking during your career? If you haven't made any major shifts, what major shifts would you like or hope to make?

2. Once you made these shifts, what became possible that seemed impossible before?

3. What was the impact of these shifts on your performance and your career?

4. How will your employees benefit from the question, "Can you separate your judgments from the facts?" Looking back at Tricia's judgments, how did this question help her think about her situation differently?

5. Look at the questions at the close of this chapter. Which of these questions would best help your employees uncover their judgments?

6. Describe an employee or a team opportunity where uncovering a judgment and helping to shift that judgment might help drive better results.

# Chapter 7

## "What's Your Problem?" -

## ATTITUDE

Our attitudes are steered directly by our judgments and feelings. Like a navigation system, attitudes set the course for the journey we take, and ultimately our final destination. If you enter the wrong information into your GPS, you will not end up where you intended. We all have the ability to control our attitudes to make sure that we arrive exactly where we want to be.

Most attitudes are generally positive or negative. We've all heard the expression, "My glass is half empty," or "I'm a glass-half-full kind of person." These attitudes are often seen as personality traits. We can also develop attitudes that are situational. Saying or thinking, "I'm sure I can finish this marathon in record time," demonstrates positivity and confidence. "Car salesmen always use trickery to make a sale," is a negative attitude, expressing feelings of suspicion.

Employees with positive attitudes—those who really care about their work—are more likely to reach goals and to succeed than those with negative attitudes or those who just show up to collect a paycheck. As a Great Manager, you should reward employees who have a positive outlook with positive recognition, as they are often your "A" players and can serve as great examples to others. When employees demonstrate a negative attitude, help them identify their judgments and shift to an attitude that will allow them to see a positive way forward.

Now, I will admit that as a manager, I've experienced an employee whose attitude always appeared positive—maybe *too* positive—to the point where it seemed phony and syrupy. A conversation with her was like eating too much chocolate and getting a stomachache. You know the type: when she asks how your weekend was and you tell her that your cat was run over, she says, "That's great! I'm so excited for you! Your kitty is in a much better place, and now you can give a needy cat a new home!" You're left wondering if she actually heard anything you said. Is there any variance on her attitude dial, or is she just on positivity auto-pilot? A phony or inauthentic positive attitude can be just as unproductive as a negative one. Invest in this type of employee the same way you would invest in one with a negative attitude, by helping that person to see the judgments that others may hold about his or her attitude, and support him or her in making a shift to a more authentic way of expressing their positivity.

While there are exceptions to the rule, a generally positive attitude contributes to success and is infectious to others.

Here are some words that may help you describe your employees' attitudes and the potential shifts that may benefit them.

Yes, but . . . What if . . . Even employees with an overall positive attitude can react negatively in certain situations, and that can keep them from taking the actions needed to get good results for themselves and for the company.

**Changing the Attitude of an Entire Team**
For almost a decade I've consulted with an extremely successful international organization with smart, capable, high-achieving executives. Their operating model had gone virtually unchanged for decades, and as an industry leader, they often set the standards that others followed. When the company was acquired by new owners, all that changed. With the new owners came restructuring and new goals, a new operating model, new partners, and new expectations. The changes were proving difficult for many longstanding employ-

ees. When the new management company began reducing the workforce it only intensified the staff's difficulty.

The leader of one of the management teams asked me to coach his group. He wanted to better understand their judgments and attitudes about the changes they were facing. My job was to help them work as a team to achieve the goals of the new owners.

The meeting was set in a beautiful beachfront hotel. The weather was great, the view was fantastic, the appointments of the hotel were spectacular, and the attitude of the participants was—well, gloomy. During our first discussion I observed that some of the eight attendees were cynical, indifferent, and even unfriendly to each other. Some were soured by the events of the past year and weren't the least bit open to the discussion or ready to move forward. I needed to help them shift their attitudes from cynical and hostile to trusting and nurturing. If this didn't happen, there would be no progress for the team, and thus, none for the company and its customers.

But during the two days we spent together, significant shifts in the team's attitudes did occur. Using the techniques of a Great Manager,

I was able to change the conversation. If you can help employees to focus on *what they appreciate*, you can change their attitudes in minutes and open up new possibilities. A negative conversation can't generate new possibilities—it can be a trap that's difficult to escape. It's not just about positive thinking, it's about helping people identify what they're grateful for but can't easily see because their attitudes are blocking their view.

Let's see how this group was able to shift their attitudes in this short conversation:

**Coach:** Help me understand your views or judgments on the changes in the business over the past year.

**Participants:**
- Communication was incredibly poor from corporate.
- I feel like we discarded the people who helped make this a great business.
- My job is completely different now!
- We're being asked to do a lot more with a lot less. There's a limit.
- The new changes make no sense. They don't know what they're doing!

**Coach:** What else?

**Participants:**
- The new executive team doesn't come from our industry.
- They're hiring MBAs right out of school! They don't know anything about our history or our business.

**Coach:** How would you characterize your own attitudes about this?

**Participants:**
- I'm mad!
- I'm fed up.
- I'm indifferent . . . it is what it is.
- It's just bad. I have a plain old bad attitude. And that's not me.

**Coach:** How is that kind of attitude serving you?

**Participants:**
- It's not!
- Not very well.
- It's not serving me—or my team, either.

**Coach:** How have you *personally* contributed to the attitudes you've just described?

**Participants:**
- Well, to be honest, I'm not sure I gave the new owners a chance.
- I guess I was angry because of some of my friends were fired.
- I think I let fear for my role overtake me. I was afraid I'd lose my job.
- I just don't like change.

**Coach:** As it relates to the changes in the business, what are you *grateful* for?

**Participants:**
- Well, I do have some new people on my team who need to be mentored and guided. I'm good at that.
- The new owners are relying on our experience to help achieve the new goals.
- I like the international expansion. I've traveled to places I'd never even heard of before.

- Right or wrong, the new leaders seem to be aligned on their vision for the company.
- There's potential for growth, and we haven't had that for a long time.
- We have new tools and resources that we've needed for a while.

**Coach:** Regarding you *personally,* what are you most grateful for?

**Participants:**
- The executive team seems to have confidence and trust in me.
- I'm learning and stretching in ways I didn't know I could.
- I can continue to provide a living for my family while doing work I enjoy.
- I can use my strengths—to learn, grow, and do new things.

**Coach**: What's at stake if we *do not, will not,* or *can not* bring this change initiative to life?

**Participants:**
- We won't be able to build the morale of our new team.
- Our entire future will be in jeopardy!
- We will become vulnerable to our competition.
- We will lose the loyalty of our customers.
- Our values are still intact, and I'd like to keep it that way.

**Coach:** Given all that you've said, what would be most valuable for you to focus on as individuals and as a team?

**Participants:**
- We will have to leverage each other's strengths—that's for sure.
- We're the leaders, and we need to demonstrate that to each other and to our team.

- If we're going to be successful, we will need to show initiative and urgency about these changes.
- We've got to give up the past and rally around the plan for the future.

**Coach:** I'm noticing a shift in your attitude. What got you energized about this discussion?

**Participants:**
- I appreciate that we're spending time together.
- It feels like we're collaborating as leaders in the business.
- This gives me a chance to think about how I can be a better leader for my team.
- This conversation helped me reset my thinking and refocus my energy.

Changes can be seen as threats *and* opportunities—they come as a set. This team found it helpful to look beyond the perceived threats and the emotions that they connected to the changes to their business. With just a few questions, they refocused and changed their attitudes. The energy in the room, the language, and the way people interacted was transformed from "Look what the new owners have done to us!" to "We've been well positioned for success and future growth." Over the years I have participated in enough of these situations with managers and leaders to assure you that these coaching conversations really work.

### It's All about *Their* Attitudes

When you're working with an employee or a team who may benefit from seeing things from a different perspective, your first instinct may be to talk about the alternatives *you* see. Resist! If you follow that instinct, you may fail to understand their judgments and they'll miss the opportunity to discover a new perspective for themselves.

Remember, your employees (just like you) are more likely to shift their perspective if they come to their own conclusions, rather than being told what to think. To help them do this, start by **identifying their attitudes** and then ask Powerful Questions:

- What does it look like to you?
- What feelings or emotions do you have?
- What is your position on this?
- If you were to take a stance, what would it be?
- How would you characterize your thoughts?

When they can see their attitudes clearly, ask Powerful Questions **to help them refocus on what's important**:

- Do you see this situation as a threat or an opportunity? Why?
- What's at stake if you hold on to your current outlook?
- How is your current attitude serving you?
- How might you think about that differently?
- How can you turn this into an opportunity?
- How can you make the most of this opportunity?
- Does the risk of failure outweigh the reward of success?
- As it relates to this situation, what are you grateful for?
- How might others view this situation?

## Worksheet for Chapter 7
## "What's Your Problem?" - ATTITUDE

1. Consider your own attitudes and how your employees may perceive them. Generally speaking, do you believe that your attitudes are seen as positive or negative?

2. How much of an impact do you believe attitude has on your team?

   1................2................3................4................5
   **No impact at all**                        **Tremendous impact**

3. Identify one judgment that you hold relating to your ability to manage your team and the individuals on it.

• What attitude do you have based on that judgment?

- How has that attitude influenced your employees and team?

4. What, if any, business results have you noticed as an outcome of your attitude, and how has that influenced your employees?

5. In the coaching dialogue in Chapter 6, we used the question, "As it relates to the changes in the business, what are you grateful for?" with a team that was clearly negative about changes in their business. What shifts did you see in the participants' attitudes after reflecting on this question?

Reread the list of Powerful Questions in this chapter. Determine which questions you can start to use immediately with your employees. Choose the ones that feel most comfortable and natural to you.

.

# Chapter 8

## "Silencing Your Inner Voice to Tell Your Story" -

## SPEECH

I like the expression, "You can't achieve it until you believe it." When we're talking about speech, that's a double-edged sword—you can achieve both desirable and undesirable results based on what you believe. Positive and negative words or phrases repeated over time build up in our minds until they become our realities, our beliefs. Speech matters! If you continuously say, "I'm bad at math," you *will* be bad at math, and others will take it as fact that you are, indeed, bad at math. The reality might be that you just don't *like* math, not that you're actually incapable of learning it. But if you say it enough, you'll undoubtedly believe it, and it will become true! Your speech, as guided by your judgments and attitudes, will have hindered your opportunity to improve your math skills.

## That Troublesome Inner Voice

> *This inner voice may not express itself audibly, but it has an enormous impact on how we view ourselves and how others view us.*

There's another form of speech that's possibly the most powerful of all—the "inner voice" inside all of us that carries our insecurities, fears, dreams, and desires. It's the voice that can hold us back or propel us forward. This inner voice may not express itself audibly, but it's often the loudest. It has an enormous impact on how we view ourselves, the way we present ourselves to others, and consequently, how others view us.

When you weave your speech together with your inner voice it becomes *your story*—the story you tell yourself and the story you tell others. This narrative takes hold and becomes the underpinning of your mindset and your reality. From this foundation, you see everything as either possible or impossible.

This inner voice places limits on us, and we must question whether those limits are real or just a story we're telling ourselves. My own practice is to challenge that inner voice—even debate and argue with it. I urge you to do the same. This requires some effort and focus, but you can reset the talk track of your inner voice and outer voice to define what's possible and reach your desired outcomes.

## The Birth of a Long-Distance Runner

A few years ago, some of my co-workers invited me to run a five-kilometer (5K) race with them in Chicago. For an experienced runner, a 5K is simple. It's easy. In fact, one guy in my office runs a 5K *every day* at lunchtime. As for me, I hadn't run since high school, and that was just so I wouldn't be late to class. My answer was an immediate "No!"

I never thought I was capable of running. My inner voice always told me, "You can't run! Your legs are too short." Or "You can't run! You're built like a fire hydrant, not an athlete." Or "You can't run with the people at work or in your neighborhood! You'll never be able to keep up." My inner voice had become a barrier—one that I myself had put up over 30 years ago. Now, for the very first time, I was aware of this barrier and the impact it was having! It upset me that I said I wasn't going to run with my co-workers. They asked me to join an activity, and I wanted to support them and participate.

Eventually I changed my answer and told my co-workers, "Count me in! I'm going to do the 5K." I decided I was going to rewrite the story for my inner voice to tell. I was going to run that 5K and I was going to have fun doing it! I started to tell myself, "You can run to the end of the block today," and I did. I said, "You can run around the neighborhood today," and I did. I said, "You can run a mile today," and I did. And so it went until, after 60 days, I was able to run over seven miles! Seven miles—*me?* I never thought that was possible, yet as soon as I started telling myself a different story, "I can't run"

changed to "I can!" "I won't be able to keep up" changed to "I will." "I'm not built to run" changed to "I am." "I'll do it" became "I did it!"

Every person has an inner voice that's telling a story that may be placing limitations on their performance. These three steps will help you uncover and address the stories that your employees are hearing:

- Listen actively to the words being said.
- Ask Powerful Questions to uncover what their inner voice is saying.
- Ask for their observations and share your own.

**Carlos's Story**

My neighbor asked me to meet with a family friend, a young man who was struggling in his first job out of college. My neighbor thought that I might be able to offer some coaching that would help this young man succeed. We met for the first time in the early morning at a diner. During my very first meeting with Carlos, I used these three steps to understand the story his inner voice was telling him. This is an excerpt from that meeting.

**Step 1: Listen actively to the words being said.**

**Gary:** Can you tell me about your role?

**Carlos:** I'm an internal marketing manager. I support a team of salespeople in the field who work directly with clients. I'm supposed to identify leads and solicit new meetings for the sales team.

**Gary:** How's that going?

**Carlos:** Not very well.

**Gary:** What makes you say that?

**Carlos:** None of my prospects answer their phone—I go straight into voicemail.

**Gary:** How many appointments are you expected to book each week?

**Carlos:** Seven is the minimum, and I get an extra incentive if I can book ten. I really want to book ten.

**Gary:** How many are you booking now?

**Carlos:** Three or four at best.

**Gary:** How are you getting those appointments?

**Carlos:** If I can get a prospective client on the phone, I can usually schedule an appointment. The problem is I can't get people to answer the phone!

**Gary:** How many attempts are you making?

**Carlos:** Well, I leave a message, sometimes two. I don't want to be a *stalker*.

**Step 2: Ask Powerful Questions to uncover what their inner voice is saying.**

**Gary:** When you continue to get voicemail instead of a live person, and you end the week with just three or four meetings, what's your attitude like?

**Carlos:** I feel like a failure! I have a list of prospective clients, and I've called every single one and only got a few people on the phone. It's useless. I'll never be able to do this! I left messages for everybody and no one returns my calls. I don't blame them. I'm just one of a hundred calls they get from pesky telemarketers every day. I'd delete my message, too, if I were them!

**Gary:** What other concerns do you have?

**Carlos:** The salespeople think I'm not doing my job, and I'm sure I'm not making a good impression on the owners, either.

**Gary:** What have they said to make you think that?

**Carlos:** Nothing—yet! But what else would they be thinking? I'm not pulling my weight, and I'm not delivering the appointments I'm supposed to!

**Step 3: Ask for their observations and share your own.**

**Gary:** If you were listening in on this conversation, what would your observations be?

**Carlos:** I'd see a guy busting his butt in a no-win situation who's about to get fired unless he can make the impossible happen!

**Gary:** May I share my observations about the story I heard from you?

**Carlos:** Please!

**Gary:** I heard that your role is to secure appointments for a team of field-based salespeople, and you do that through phone solicitations. When you get potential candidates on the phone, you're usually successful in confirming a meeting. However, you believe that people don't answer their phones because they get messages from lots of marketers, and you're no different. I also heard you say that if you call too often, you would be seen as a stalker. In addition, you feel like a failure because you're not producing ten appointments a week, and that you believe the sales team and owners have a negative impression of you. Did I get your thoughts accurately?

**Carlos:** Yes, that sums it all up pretty well! Pathetic, don't you think?

This is an accurate account of how one person's speech and inner voice came together to create a personal story—one that he thought would end in failure or on the unemployment line.

The story that Carlos was telling himself was a major obstacle to his success. His speech and inner voice gave great insights into his judgments, attitudes, and even detailed the future he saw for himself in this position: "I'd see a guy busting his butt in a no-win situation who's about to get fired unless he can make the impossible happen!"

By helping people change that inner voice and their speech, you can alter the ending of stories like this. As a Great Manager, you can turn this story around and achieve a positive result for your employee, the team, and the company.

Now, let's get back to that conversation:

**Gary:** What did you notice about the language you used to describe your work situation?

**Carlos:** I thought my words were honest and direct. They described how I really feel.

**Gary:** I took some notes on the words you used to tell your story. May I read them back to you?

**Carlos:** Okay . . .

**Gary:** Here's what I heard:

- Not very well!
- I can't get people on the phone.
- I don't want to be a stalker.
- I feel like a failure!
- There's no way for me to book these meetings.
- It's useless.
- I'll never be able to do this.
- I'm just one of a hundred calls from pesky telemarketers.
- I'd delete my message if I were them.
- The salespeople don't think I'm doing my job.
- I'm not making a good impression on the owners.
- I'm not pulling my weight.
- I'm not delivering the appointments I'm supposed to!

- A no-win situation.
- I'm about to get fired if I don't make the impossible happen!
- Pathetic!

So let me ask you again—what did you notice about the words you used to describe your work situation?

**Carlos:** Wow! I didn't realize what a bad attitude I have! It's kind of shocking to hear all of those words read back to me.

**Gary:** How do you think these things you've been telling yourself have affected your performance?

**Carlos:** It can't be good, that's for sure!

**Gary:** Can you say some more about that?

**Carlos:** Well, if that's what's really going on in my head, there's not a lot of room for anything else!

**Gary:** Would it be worthwhile for us to talk about this some more?

**Carlos:** Yes! Yes, it would.

So, during the conversation that followed, we discussed **judgments**—how many calls he believed he should make to meet his quota, his ability to create new ways to approach prospects, the way others perceived him, and his potential to be successful in this role. We also talked about how his **attitude**, as dictated by his inner voice, was steering his performance and the viability of the work, and how this defeatist attitude was holding him back from thinking of innovative and alternative ways to reach potential buyers. And we talked about his **speech**—the story he was telling himself and how it was becoming a reality—as well as his ability to rewrite it so he could become more productive and successful.

As a Great Manager, you can help your employees to rewrite their stories. Together, you can deconstruct the stories to identify their existing speech and inner voice. Then, you can help them replace speech that blocks success with speech that moves them forward.

The new story should include the desired results, the actions it will take to attain them, and the attitude that will support both of these.

Here's how Carlos rewrote his story through his speech and inner voice:

**Gary:** Now that you see how your speech is impacting your success, what is the story you want to create?

**Carlos:** I want to create a story that gets rid of the roadblocks and focuses on success.

**Coach:** Take some time to start to write your new story. Using "I will," "I can," and "I am" as sentence starters, write down these things:

- The results you want to achieve.
- The actions you'll need to take to achieve them.
- The attitude that will support them both.

After several trials Carlos wrote this story:

I'm successful at converting conversations to appointments. I'll secure ten sales appointments a week by increasing the number of conversations I have. I'll do this by increasing my outbound call activity to 100 a day, and I can follow up through email and social media to reach people who prefer to communicate online.

With this statement, he was already beginning to shift his perspective, and he was discovering new possibilities that he couldn't see before, as well as planning actions that he'd never considered.

**Powerful Questions to uncover speech and the inner voice:**
- Can you say more about that?
- What makes you think that?
- Why do you say that?
- What do you think?
- How would you describe your current thinking?
- What are you telling yourself?

- What's the story that you would tell others?
- What's holding you back?
- What successes have you had?

# Worksheet for Chapter 8
## "Silencing Your Inner Voice to Tell Your Story" - SPEECH

1. What words have you either said out loud or through your inner voice that you believe have supported your success?

2. How has your speech held you back? What words have you used to reinforce a negative attitude?

3. Asking Carlos to write a new story using "I will," "I can," and "I am," enabled him to design a new future for himself. Using statements beginning with these words, create your own future as a Great Manager.

4. Review the Powerful Questions in this chapter. What additional Powerful Questions might you ask your employees or team to uncover their speech and inner voice? Write at least three.

   •

   •

   •

5. Helping your employees recognize the speech that supports their success or holds them back requires you to be an active listener. What can you do to demonstrate active listening? Here are a few tips to get you started. Add some of your own:

- Maintain eye contact while you're talking.
- Use gestures, such as nodding your head, to show you understand.
- Paraphrase what you hear and ask clarifying questions.

# Chapter 9

## "All of You" -

## PHYSICALITY

As a Great Manager, you regard each employee as a whole person, and understand that speech is only a small portion of what that person is telling you and what you are hearing.

While choice of words is undoubtedly important, it's only one piece of our communication. Tone of voice is important, and nonverbal behaviors such as facial expressions can be more powerful than words. Judgments, attitudes, and speech can—and will—greatly influence the facial expressions, body movements, posture, and gestures—the physical elements of speech.

What does this mean for the Great Manager? It means that you'll become an observer of your employees' physical presence and share your assessments of their physicality. These observations are important not just for the coaching conversation, but for helping employees better comprehend how they are projecting themselves to others. You can help them to see how their physical being is either aiding or hindering their actions and relaying both positive and negative attitudes.

Asking Powerful Questions about employees' physical presence doesn't have to be limited to how it may be holding them back. These questions can also establish what's working well and how to apply that in other situations.

Kirsten is an up-and-coming marketing executive whose success is highly dependent on her presentation skills. Her senior marketing director, Travis, accompanies her to a big presentation for a potential client, and is very pleased with how she engages her audience. After the meeting they walk to the parking lot together and debrief the meeting. Let's have a look.

**Travis:** Your presentation seemed to be really well received! You made eye contact with everyone in the room during your talk.

**Kirsten:** Wow, you noticed that? It's funny, I just read an article about the importance of making eye contact during presentations and I thought I'd try it today.

**Travis:** So what did you notice?

**Kirsten:** I thought the group was totally engaged, like they were really interested in what I had to say!

**Travis:** I noticed the same thing. They were hanging on your every word! Did you notice anything else?

**Kirsten:** Yeah—I was really able to read the room today and adjust my presentation based on the reactions I saw on people's faces. I got a lot more questions than I normally do at these meetings; they got really involved.

**Travis:** Where else do you think you might try this?

**Kirsten:** You know, I was making an extra effort because I wanted to land this new account. I really should use the same technique to engage my existing clients, too. Sometimes I show up at a client to present a marketing campaign and I am totally focused on my presentation slides. I've got to pay more attention to the client's reactions and less time staring at the slides.

**Travis:** Keep me posted—I'm sure you are going to close a lot more deals based on the way you worked the room today!

When I was a young manager in the food service industry, I was very excited to tell Maria, an hourly employee, that she was getting a raise for her great performance and progress over the previous few months.

When she first started, Maria seemed to lack self-confidence. She walked around with her head down and avoided eye contact with me and everyone else. She was a hard worker, but she made very little conversation with co-workers or customers, and she didn't seem to be having any fun. She came to work, did her job, and then went home. While Maria was an effective and drama-free employee, I sensed she was not working up to her potential. As the months passed, Maria started to gain confidence and came out of her shell. Soon, she was talking more, making eye contact, walking around with her head held high, and becoming a well-rounded employee.

We were really busy on the day I planned to tell her about the raise. In the middle of a rush of customers, I hurried past her in the back hallway of the restaurant and said, "Maria, I want to talk to you at the end of the day. Can you stick around for a few minutes when you finish your shift?" She said she would.

During the rest of that that day, Maria had her head down again. She seemed withdrawn. Had I been wrong about the progress I thought I'd seen over the past few months? Was I making a mistake in giving her a raise? How could I recognize her for her progress if she was looking at the floor again and acting detached? I was filled with doubt as her workday came to a close. Here's what happened:

**Gary:** Maria, do you still have time to talk?
**Maria:** Ugh. I guess so.
**Gary:** What's the matter with you? You've been moping around staring at the ground all day.
**Maria:** I can't afford to lose this job! You know I have two kids at home!
**Gary:** *What?*
**Maria:** I've been doing my best for months, and I thought you were happy with me. I was really starting to like it here, too. I can't believe you're firing me! You've been a really nice boss, and all my other managers have been real jerks!
**Gary:** Firing you? Where did you get that idea?

**Maria:** This morning you flew past me and you said you wanted to talk to me at the end of the day. You didn't even look at me. You *never* ask to talk to me at the end of the day! What else could it be?

**Gary:** Oh, no! Is *that* why you've been dragging around all day? I wanted to tell you what a great job you were doing! I wanted to offer you a raise based on all your hard work. I don't want to fire you—I want to give you a raise!

**Maria:** *Really?* (The tears that were flowing were from joy and re-lief.)

**Gary:** Really!

Looking back, I'm still sensitive about the fact that she suffered through an entire day in fear of losing her job. Knowing what I know now, the moment I saw her physicality revert back to her old ways, I should have offered my observations, asked her about it, and saved her eight hours of worry.

What is physically communicated to others is almost entirely influenced by judgments, attitudes, and speech. For some, it will show up as rigidity of the lower back, tension in the chest, or shallow or rapid

> *The changes in your physicality may be telling an unintentional story to those around you. This can send messages that you really don't want or intend to project.*

breathing. For others, it can manifest as poor posture, sagging shoulders, and a lowered head. These physical reactions limit oxygen to the brain and hamper our ability to think clearly about new solutions and new possibilities. At the same time, the changes in your physicality may be telling an unintentional story to those around you. They may perceive you as frustrated, unhappy, isolated, and unapproachable. This physicality may send confusing or negative messages that you really don't want to project.

Over time, if these negative physical manifestations aren't corrected, they can become habits. The body can quickly come to recognize stress as the norm, adopting the rolled-over shoulders and absence of eye contact as customary behavior. As a Great Manager, observing the physical presence of your employees and offering your observations will help them recognize what they are communicating to others. With this insight and perspective, your employees can adjust their physicality and project the story they truly want to tell.

Years ago, after completing my first year with a new company, I met with my manager for my annual review. I was anxious to hear all of the accolades of which I felt so deserving! After all, I was the only person in our small company to hit bonus that year. I had transitioned into my new role with ease, and had added financial value and thought leadership to the business. I appeared to be a very good cultural fit with the company. While I wasn't quite *gloating,* I was feeling very confident as I walked into this review—and with good reason.

As expected, the review—which included peer feedback—highlighted my accomplishments. However, I hadn't expected the attention given to my needs for improvement! The review had been going along just fine until I read this comment from a co-worker: "Sometimes in meetings, Gary will roll his eyes at certain suggestions or statements, clearly signaling that he doesn't agree with or value what is being said. It seems disrespectful."

That comment rattled me to my core! I didn't realize I was rolling my eyes! How long had I been doing this? Who felt offended? Is this something I could actually control? I was aware, for the first time (and in a very palpable way), what I was communicating with my physicality. I never wanted to communicate disrespect. I may have been saying the right things and delivering the expected results, but apparently I was also sending a message that people perceived as disrespect. If I continued this, it could eventually undermine all of my positive intent, efforts, and results. I realized that success in the workplace had as much to do with how I showed up physically as with what I contributed to the bottom line.

As a Great Manager, you have a unique opportunity to identify how your employees' judgments, attitudes, and speech are affecting their bodies. A simple and Powerful Question such as, "How is that showing up in your body?" can take your employees on a trip inside their physical being. When they recognize and identify how their body is reacting to situations, they make the first step to taking control of the story they are telling themselves and others.

I want to be very clear about dealing with the physical presence of an employee. As a Great Manager, you need to limit your observations, questions, and comments to those that are appropriate within social boundaries and the professional standards of your business. When you're trying to explain to someone what their body is telling people, don't touch—demonstrate. Your job as a Great Manager is to coach, not have a complaint filed against you by HR. *Show* that person the physicality you're observing, such as posture or facial expressions. Also, avoid observations based on personal opinion or preferences. "Hey—you have the same hairstyle as my poodle!" is an example of an observation based on a personal opinion, and one that's best kept to yourself.

Your focus is appropriate in the three observable physical domains. Let's explore them.

**Three Observable Physical Domains**

| Facial Expressions | Body Movements and Posture | Gestures |
|---|---|---|
| The eyes, eyebrows, eyelids, head, and mouth work together to show commonly recognized expressions: | The motions of the arms, legs, torso, shoulders, back, and head transmit a message to others: | The hands, arms, head, and face can articulate a full range of messages: |
| Fear | Happiness | Hello |
| Interest | Sadness | Okay |
| Disinterest | Impatience | Wait a minute |
| Sadness | Calmness | Yes |
| Anger | Eagerness | No |
| Joy | Excitement | Come here |
| Surprise | Disappointment | I don't know |
| Disgust | Lethargy | I don't care |
| Shame | Anxiety | Stay away |

While these domains are *outward* expressions, physical manifestations of our judgments, attitudes, and speech can also be *internal* or less noticeable. One of the easiest and most effective ways to help your employees is to notice their breathing—how rapid, shallow, or deep it is. The tightening of the chest, lower back pain, and a "nervous stomach" are all physical but not necessarily observable. Asking your employees about their physicality—whether you notice anything or not—is a part of coaching your employee to success. Don't worry—you're not (nor should you be!) attempting to be a doctor or a physical therapist. You're becoming a Great Manager, and that alone may be therapeutic for you, your employee, and your team.

If I could go back in time and re-do my talk with Maria, I'd be much more aware of her physicality and my own. When I rushed in to say that I wanted to talk to her, I was most likely harried, and I'm sure my body language and gestures told her that I wanted to leave quickly. I can now easily see how she could have interpreted the speed of my message and my quick movements as discomfort about having to fire her. With that premise, she quickly reverted to her old characteristics and began to protect herself from what she expected by withdrawing from yet another negative manager conversation.

If I could do it again, I would have started a coaching conversation months earlier, and our talk would have gone like this:

**Gary:** Hey, Maria, do you have a few minutes to talk? I want to find out how you're doing in your new position.

**Maria:** I'm okay. Things are fine, I think. Did I do something wrong?

**Gary:** Not at all! I think you're really working hard. How do you think things are going?

**Maria:** I've been keeping my head down, staying focused, and trying to stay out of trouble.

**Gary:** You certainly are focused! I want to understand what you mean by "trouble." Can you say some more about that?

**Maria:** I know how bosses hate to be bothered, so I'm trying to figure stuff out without bugging you.

**Gary:** You can ask me questions anytime! In fact, I want you to ask me questions so you have the information you need to do a great job. When have you had a manager who thought you were bothering him or her with questions?

**Maria:** I had this one manager that yelled a lot. He'd get really mad if you came into his office and asked questions. He made us all feel pretty stupid for not knowing everything.

**Gary:** That's rough. I'm sorry—that must have been a terrible experience. I have noticed that when I'm around, you tend to look down and don't make eye contact with me. Why do you think that is?

**Maria:** Like I said, I am trying to stay out of trouble. I did my best to stay off my last manager's radar; I got used to avoiding him as much as I could. I just kept my head down—literally. I did my work and kept to myself so I didn't get on his bad side.

**Gary:** So you always had your head down. That's a significant physical response. What else did you notice about how you physically reacted to that situation?

**Maria:** I was always nervous. I walked around with a lump in my throat that was so bad I couldn't even eat lunch at work. I always waited until I got home to eat. I was in knots!

**Gary:** To me it looks like you're still in knots. I'm curious if you think that others might notice that too?

**Maria:** I'm not sure. What do you think?

**Gary:** I can't speak for everyone, but you don't seem very comfortable here. I don't see you having any fun with your co-workers or our customers; I'd love to see you add some enjoyment to your hard work! If it's okay, I'd like to talk with you a bit about how I operate as a manager. I think you'll find that things here are a lot different from your previous job.

**Maria:** Okay! I really do like it here, and want to get to know people. I don't want to give the wrong impression. Having fun at work sounds good to me.

What strikes me now—with the benefit of 20 years' hindsight, valuable training, and role modeling—is what an inexperienced manager I was! Having had no Great Manager role model, I was focused on the wrong things. I never shared my observations, and that's key to being a good coach. I waited for good things to happen, and when they did, I focused on the rewards that I could give or the positive messages I could share. I didn't know enough to engage my employees and elicit information about why they might be unhappy or performing below capacity.

For yesterday's manager, employees' physicality pertained solely to their ability to perform their work. Concerns over a broken arm, a pulled muscle, or the flu—and possible absence from work or impact on duties—were (and often still are) the only reasons for a conversation about physical being. Great Managers are, of course, concerned about these same issues, but at the same time, they also recognize that an employee's physicality is an important communication tool. In fact, an employee who sulks and shows visible stress may very well be less productive than a motivated, engaged employee with a pulled muscle or a cold. A Great Manager engages his team to uncover the source and effect of physicality so everyone can perform effectively and successfully.

As a Great Manager, you ask Powerful Questions to understand the story that your employees are telling through their physicality and to help them recognize how others might interpret them. You help them gain insights into how their physicality might be getting in the way of the actions that will deliver the desired results. You offer your observations about how their facial expressions, body movements, posture, or gestures are propelling them forward, and you ask them how they might leverage that for continued success.

**Powerful Questions to Address Physicality:**

- How is that showing up for you physically?
- What are you observing about your:
  - ✦ Facial expressions?
  - ✦ Body movements and posture?
  - ✦ Gestures?
- What do you think others perceive by observing your physical presence?
- If you could put a voice to your body movement, what would it say?
- How are you telling that story through your physicality?

## Worksheet for Chapter 9
## "All of You" - PHYSICALITY

1. Just as you will need to become an observer of your employees' physical presence, they are observers of yours. Looking through your employees' eyes, what do you think they notice about your physical presence?

2. Referring to the "Three Observable Physical Domains," identify at least one from each category that best represents you. What conclusions could others draw from your facial expressions, body movements and posture, and gestures?

3. How has your physicality potentially held you back? How has it supported your success?

4. In the story about Maria, we learned that her physicality was directly impacted by her previous work experiences and that it improved as she became more confident. During the next interactions with your employees, pay particular attention to their physicality and document your observations.

**Employee Observations**

| Facial Expressions | Body Movements and Posture | Gestures |
|---|---|---|
|  |  |  |
|  |  |  |
|  |  |  |

5. Review "Powerful Questions to Address Physicality." Identify which ones you are most likely to use and/or develop a few of your own. What question or questions will you use to discover what's behind your employees' physicality?

# Chapter 10

## "Actions That Deliver Results" -

## ACTIONS

Action is the culmination and outward response to information. All of our judgments, attitudes, speech, and physicality combine to influence the steps we will or will not take. If even one of these elements is out of alignment with the others, it could mean that our actions may not deliver the expected or desired results.

Without very deliberate action, desired results are just that—desire, not reality. Judgments, attitudes, speech, and physicality come together to act as an actual barricade to action for some employees. Others, with the best of intentions, will take actions that don't deliver the desired results for them, their team, or the organization.

And still others will actually take the actions that deliver the desired results.

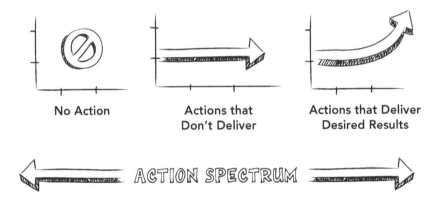

No Action     Actions that Don't Deliver     Actions that Deliver Desired Results

ACTION SPECTRUM

**Let's consider an example of each of the three areas on this spectrum:**

**No Action:**
"I want to win the Salesman of the Year award, but I'm concerned that this year's sales goals are so unrealistic that they are just not achievable."

**Judgment**: Sales goals are unrealistic.
**Attitude**: Defeatist.
**Speech**: "They are just not achievable."
**Physicality**: Subtle slump in posture.
**Actions**: None.
**Likely Results**: None.

People can become focused on the *barriers* that they believe prevent them from making progress, instead of focusing on what they *can* make happen. As a Great Manager, you must guide your employee to think about what is possible without the barriers they have created, such as the defeatist attitude in this example. Using the JASPAR methodology, you can redirect your employees away from self-imposed barriers that limit and inhibit performance. When you help them to think about what is possible without barriers, they can challenge their beliefs and take action.

### Actions That Don't Deliver Results

"I want to win the Salesperson of the Year award! Raising all of my prices will increase my sales number. That award is going to be mine!"

**Judgment**: Raising prices will increase the sales number.
**Attitude**: Overconfident, superior.
**Speech**: "That award is going to be mine!"
**Physicality**: Hands clasped behind head, reclining with legs crossed.
**Actions**: All prices are raised.
**Likely Result**: Sales number actually drops because of the price increase.

Employees can be very passionate about the actions they take, truly believing that they are doing everything right. However, even good intentions can lead to undesired outcomes. If those passionate actions are not leading to the desired outcomes, you can help employees make a shift by asking them to step back and view the situation as an observer. As an observer they may be able to see how the actions they believe are right are actually counterproductive, and come up with solutions they may have not considered.

### Actions that Deliver Desired Results

"I want to win the Salesperson of the Year award! I will find ways to provide more value to my existing accounts, add new accounts, and establish myself as a trusted advisor to both."

**Judgment**: Adding more value to customers and being a trusted advisor will increase sales.

**Attitude**: Confident and excited.

**Speech**: "I will find ways to provide more value."

**Physicality**: Good posture, chest out, head upright.

**Actions**: Works with existing customers to help solve their business problems, and calls on potential new accounts daily to build new relationships. Attends industry events, and reads articles to become an expert on trends that impact customers.

**Likely Result**: Increases business with existing clients, adds new clients, is a trusted advisor to both—and wins the award.

In addition to the appropriate reward and recognition, a Great Manager helps employees recognize the judgments, attitudes, speech, and physicality that contribute to their actions, and in turn, to the desired results. By advising the employee that his focus on adding value was more effective than raising prices, you enable him to maximize his contribution. The result is more efficient work performance and an improved bottom line. Using this method helps employees to deliver results that are both repeatable and sustainable. This will help them understand what has worked well and will reinforce success routines for the future.

## My Own "Aha!"

When coaching others, I use the following example to explain how we can unintentionally get in the way of actions and inhibit desired results with negative judgments, attitudes, speech, and physicality.

On a trip to visit a potential client in Arizona, I landed hours before my meeting, with plenty of time to spare. I had waited months to meet with the board of a major corporation, and I was well prepared for an important presentation.

I decided to drive around and see some sights before heading to my client's office building. At some point, I became distracted and realized that I had driven in the wrong direction for over 30 minutes! Even though I turned around immediately, I knew I was going to be late. If I missed this opportunity to present, it could be months before I'd get another chance—if ever. I was sure I was about to lose the trust of a company that I had spent the past year building.

I began to tell myself, "I'm going to be late! They'll never trust me again. This deal is as good as dead." Then, I stopped myself in mid-judgment. Just as I was breaking into a sweat, I asked myself, "How can you still make this meeting?" I came up with three different actions that could potentially have saved the meeting.

I immediately called my contact at the client's office to tell him my circumstance and the actions I had thought of to solve the problem. Before I could explain, he said, "Gary, I was just about to call you. I'm really sorry, but the board meeting is running long. Can we push your presentation back about an hour?" My reply was very calm and cheerful: "Sure! I'm happy to accommodate the board's schedule. See you in a bit!"

Call it what you will, but by the time luck, fate, or chance took over, I had already shifted my judgment. My attitude had changed, and my speech was moving me toward solutions. The physical stress had passed, and my course of action became clear. Now, my desired results and the actual results had become one: I would be on time for the meeting! So while I had the lucky break of an unplanned delay, I was already on my way to achieving my desired result because I took control of my attitude and speech, resulting in positive action.

What if I hadn't made this shift? What if I hadn't taken action and called the client? The scenarios are endless, but I do have the picture in my mind of seeing a police car in my rearview mirror, sirens blaring and lights flashing, with a burly patrolman ready to nail me for speeding. Besides making myself even later for the appointment, I'd have had to explain yet another ticket to my wife, which would be far worse, and that wasn't my desired result.

**Teaching Employees to Fish**

Your role as a Great Manager is to observe and understand where your employees' actions fall on the action spectrum, and then ask Powerful Questions to uncover how they got to that point.

The difference in the approach between an ordinary manager and a Great Manager is the difference between giving someone a fish so that person can eat for a day, versus teaching him or her to fish so he or she can eat for life. Managers who just give employees answers spend much of their time telling—*giving* them a fish. A Great Manager asks Powerful Questions about how or why actions are being taken. This gives employees the opportunity to discover how they can consistently make decisions that align with the desired results in the future—*teaching* them to fish.

Over time, your employees will be able to ask *themselves* Powerful Questions and more easily assess their current actions. This type of empowerment gives them the ability to grow their skills and confidence. Your interaction with those empowered and confident employees will still be needed, and you may find that your coaching partnership and conversations grow richer over time. By "teaching your employees to fish," you are indeed developing the next generation of Great Managers.

Sanjay is a managing partner in a large management consulting firm. Matt is a junior consultant who has been assigned to a high-profile client that is known for being high demand and high maintenance. Matt has received some tough feedback from his client and is very quick to ask for some counsel from Sanjay. Before they are able to schedule a meeting time, they happen to pass each other in the hallway of their office. Let's listen in.

**Sanjay:** Hey, Matt. I saw your email and I was going to schedule some time with you later this afternoon, but I have a few minutes now if you want to talk.

**Matt:** I'm just coming back from lunch, and I have about 30 minutes before my next meeting. I think we can fit this in now.

**Sanjay:** Let's head to the conference room where we can have some privacy.

Once Sanjay and Matt have settled in, Sanjay starts the coaching conversation by finding out what's most important for Matt to talk about.

**Sanjay:** Your email said that you wanted to discuss one of your accounts. What, specifically, do you want to talk about?

**Matt:** Sanjay, I got some really tough feedback from Jonathan at the ACME account. He said that he's lost confidence in me and in my ability to keep my commitments. He lost confidence in me, that's a joke! His expectations are crazy! Maybe you should see if someone else can handle this lunatic any better than I can. I can't deal with him anymore.

**Sanjay:** Now, wait a minute—let's talk it through before we jump to conclusions. Can we agree that we want the best outcome for the client, our business, and you?

**Matt:** Fair enough—I was just blowing off steam!

**Sanjay:** What expectations were set with Jonathan?

**Matt:** We had project reviews scheduled for every Friday morning during the project-development timeline.

**Sanjay:** What were the outcomes of those reviews?

**Matt:** Over the past three reviews, Jonathan has said that he's not happy with my work. You know how demanding this client is! He gives us unrealistic amounts of work that we can't possibly finish on time. It's impossible to meet his deadlines, and I've been putting in 60 hour weeks! I'm exhausted.

**Sanjay:** I can see that you're tired. So tell me . . . what's really happening—based on actual facts—and what are the judgments you added to your story?

**Matt:** I don't think I'm adding anything to what is really happening. The guy is impossible, and that's a fact. He's totally unreasonable in his requests, and that's also a fact! There is nothing humanly possible that I can do to get this work done in time and satisfy him. I give up. I just give up!

**Sanjay:** Okay . . . so let me ask that question a different way. What has the customer identified as the specific points of dissatisfaction?

**Matt:** He says that the work is late and not up to his standards.

**Sanjay:** So far, I've heard you say that the client is demanding, unrealistic, impossible, and completely unreasonable. I also heard you say that the work has been late and not up to the customer's standards. Did I hear you correctly?

**Matt:** Yes.

**Sanjay:** May I offer my observations?

**Matt:** Yes! That's why I'm talking to you!

**Sanjay:** It sounds like your attitude is one of defeat. I hear that you've declared this customer to be impossible to satisfy, and that you've given up. Matt, look at the speech you're using to describe the customer. When you combine that with your exhaustion and the fact that you've already claimed defeat, I don't see how you can possibly come up with any ideas on how to satisfy Jonathan.

**Matt:** You've got a point. But I still don't think there is any way to please him.

**Sanjay:** For a moment, remove everything that's in your way—your current judgments about Jonathan, your attitude of defeat, your negative speech, and even your physical exhaustion. Just push them aside. If nothing were in your way and you knew it would all turn out well, what would you do to change this situation?

**Matt:** Nothing in the way? Well, I'd start by asking for longer deadlines.

**Sanjay:**  What else?

**Matt:**  I would ask to expand the budget so we could bring on another partner to help ensure the quality of the work.

**Sanjay:**  What's holding you back from doing just that?

**Matt:**  To tell you the truth, Sanjay, I didn't take the time to think about it.  Even now, I'm skeptical that Jonathan will go for any of these ideas.

**Sanjay:**  I understand that you're skeptical, but are you willing to take action and reach out to him?

**Matt:**  Why not, the worst that can happen is that he can say no or think that I am an idiot for asking.  He's already unhappy with me, so I don't have much to lose here.  If I need you, would you join me on a call with Jonathan to discuss this?

**Sanjay:**  Of course I will.  I suggest that you get this conversation started ASAP, because another deadline will be here before you know it.

**Matt:**  I'll send him an email when I get back to my desk.  I'll let you know if I need you.  Thanks, Sanjay.


Can you see how Matt's judgments, attitude, speech, and physical exhaustion led to inaction and poor results?  Until he removed those barriers, Matt was unable to take action, because the mind and body work together to either enable or prevent action.  Matt's manager—a Great Manager—asked a few Powerful Questions to help Matt identify actions that might create the results that he and his customer wanted.


Here are more Powerful Questions to use when you're talking about actions that might be helpful:

- Are there additional actions you could be taking?
- Are you ready and willing to take the actions we've discussed?
- What is your plan?
- Are the actions you're taking getting you the results you want?

- How have your judgments influenced your actions?
- How has your attitude affected your actions and results?
- How are the actions you're taking serving you?
- If the barriers you mentioned were gone, what actions could you take?

## Worksheet for Chapter 10
### "Actions That Deliver Results" - ACTIONS

1.  As a manager, how have your own judgments, attitudes, speech, and physicality influenced your ability to take action?

2.  Think about a time when you were able to remove some of the barriers that your judgments, attitudes, speech, and physicality have caused. What did you do, and how did that feel?

3.  Now, think of a time when you were *not* able to remove those barriers. What did it feel like—taking no action or taking the wrong action?

4. Choose an individual employee or your entire team. Document the judgments, attitudes, speech, and physicality you've observed when the employee or team took no action, actions that failed to deliver results, or actions that resulted in desired results.

| | No Actions | Actions that Don't Deliver Desired Results | Actions that Deliver Desired Results |
|---|---|---|---|
| Judgments | | | |
| Attitude | | | |
| Speech | | | |
| Physicality | | | |

5. Next, select one scenario from this chart and plan a coaching conversation to address it. Use the Powerful Questions you've learned, and choose one or more question from each chapter to use in your conversation. Good luck!

# Chapter 11

## "As Seen on TV!" –

## RESULTS –

## Desired and Actual

I know you've seen one of those television infomercials touting a great new weight-loss or exercise product. There is invariably a "before" picture of one of their satisfied customers followed by an "after" picture showing a half-naked, glistening, super-slim sports model. In most cases, I'd be happy to just look like the "before" picture! But they're promising desired results. And at the bottom of the screen, a message appears: *Actual results may vary*. And boy, *do* they!

Results are at the core of your commitment to your company, your team, and your individual employees. They are the measures by which you are rewarded, and likely the way your team and employees receive their recognition as well.

In your business, actual results may vary from desired results, as well. In your role as a Great Manager, you'll need to highlight the gap between desired and actual results and coach your employees to bridge that gap.

The two categories of results—desired and actual—have equal importance for you as a Great Manager. Desired results are the outcomes we *want* to achieve, and actual results are the outcomes that we *end up with.* Ideally, they match perfectly—but all too often, that's not the case. Desired results and actual results can be very different because . . . *results may vary.*

> *You may believe that you have provided everything people need to take actions that lead to desired results. But what's really important is what your employees believe!*

As a Great Manager, you know that achieving desired results is almost solely based on the actions taken by your employees. You may believe that you or your organization has provided everything people need to take actions that lead to desired results. However, what is really important is what your *employees* believe! Their judgments, attitudes, speech, and physicality affect their actions, and thus, your ability as a manager to deliver results.

To deliver desired results, you'll need to use all four of these steps: Establish desired results, ask Powerful Questions, create shifts, and review the desired results. Let's see how this works.

The first step is to establish desired results for the organization as well as for the employee. Every company initiative is a chance to connect individual goals with the goals of the organization, making it the ideal place to start. Your employees also have goals and aspirations, both work-related and individual. The more you can help them reach these aspirations through your company's goals, the more likely that desired results and actual results will match.

Justin, a call-center customer service associate, considers himself to be an expert at his job and has strong ideas about how things should be done within the customer service department. His manager, Phil, is part of a team that is working on a new customer service initiative for the company. This initiative, if successful, could result in an improved customer experience, increased associate effectiveness, and great job satisfaction. Phil knows that Justin can influence others on his team, and wants to talk to him about helping to launch the initiative to ensure the desired results are achieved. Let's join Phil as he approaches Justin at his cubicle to have a coaching conversation to *establish desired results*:

**Phil:** Hey Justin, you know the new customer service initiative that I've been working on . . . I want to talk about it with you, is this a good time?

**Justin:** I need to grab some lunch; can we talk in my car while I hit the drive-thru window?

**Phil:** Sure. I'll grab a bite with you. You drive, I'll buy.

**Justin:** Deal! So, you're finally ready to spill beans about the new customer service initiative. Tell me about it. What's going to change?

**Phil:** Our first goal is to improve our customer satisfaction scores by five percent in the next three months. We've taken a look at the customer surveys and it's no shock that callers would be much happier if we reduced their on-hold time. What was a surprise on our scores was how accurately they believed we handled their calls. It was much lower than we had anticipated.

**Justin:** I could have told you that! Most calls I take start with the customer *yelling* because we put them on hold or because we didn't help during their last call. I spend more time apologizing than helping.

**Phil:** That doesn't sound like a lot of fun. What if we could improve our scores? What would that mean to you personally?

**Justin:** It's not just about the score, Phil. There is actually a customer on the other end of the phone line, and that person is usually yelling at those of us on this end of the phone. We'd all be a heck of a lot happier if we could just help customers solve problems and not have them yell at us—now that would be huge! So, how are we going to make this happen?

The next step for Phil in this conversation is to **Ask Powerful Questions** so he can better understand Justin's judgments, attitudes, speech, physicality, and actions. This may give him an immediate understanding of the potential barriers in reaching the desired results. Great Managers are proactive in these conversations!

As Phil and Justin pull away from the drive-thru window, their conversation continues. Let's see how Phil uses Powerful Questions in his talk with Justin:

**Phil:** The new plan uses technology to leverage the problem-resolution talents of our team. We're installing an automated customer service routing software that allows callers to specify the type of problem they are having. We'll segment the call-center staff into areas of expertise, and everyone will have a specialty in different areas of problem resolution. When a call comes in to one of our associates, they will already know what it's related to and they will have the expertise to resolve the problem quickly and accurately. We believe this will lead to a dramatic increase in customer satisfaction. What do you think about it?

**Justin:** I think we should leave well enough alone. When you've been here as long as I have, you see a lot. Our leaders come and go, but I'm still here, and I'm telling you this won't work!

**Manager:** Hmm. It sounds like you don't have a lot of faith in the plan. What, if anything, do you *like* about it?

**Justin:**  Well, the part about being able to focus on a specific area is good.  I kind of like being an expert.

**Manager:**  Justin, as someone who's been here a long time, what worries you about this plan?

**Justin:**  Well, our customers constantly complain about getting lost in the phone system and having to deal with recordings before they get a live person.  It's confusing and frustrating and I don't blame them!  By the sounds of it, we aren't addressing that issue at all—in fact, we might be making it worse!

By asking Powerful Questions, a Great Manager **Creates Shifts** as needed to remove the barriers to taking the actions that deliver the desired results.  These barriers may show up as judgments, attitudes, speech, or physicality.  Through Powerful Questions, Phil must now help Justin identify new perspectives and create shifts in his thinking to help him overcome his skepticism.  Without a new perspective it is unlikely that Justin will buy into the changes ahead.  Let's check in on Justin and Phil as they pull into the parking lot of their office and continue to talk:

**Phil:**  So Justin, is it your belief that *any* automated system will confuse and frustrate customers?

**Justin:**  Yes!  I've *never* worked with an automated phone system that I liked, and I've been in this industry a long time.

**Phil:**  What's the end result you'd like to see for our customers?

**Justin:**  I want them to have the quickest, most accurate problem-resolution possible without getting lost in a phone system.  I want them to reach me easily and without frustration.  I want to start a conversation without being yelled at.

**Phil:**  Yeah, I know that dealing with frustrated customers has got to be the most difficult part of your job.

**Justin:** Dealing with frustrated customers comes with the territory, but I don't like getting yelled at, and it sounds like that's not going to change.

**Phil:** May I offer you my observations?

**Justin:** I know, I know . . . I'm being a real pain.

**Phil:** I was actually noticing how passionate you are about serving our customers. That matches perfectly with the desired results we're trying to achieve. I've also noticed that you have a very broad judgment against automated phone systems, but no specific experience with the system we're going to implement. It sounds like you've already made up your mind that the new system isn't going to reduce the frustration of our customers.

**Justin:** Wow, Boss, that's some harsh feedback, but I have to admit, it is what I said.

**Phil:** If you were watching this conversation, what would your observations be?

**Justin:** Well, as you said, I'd see someone who is passionate about the customer and who's had some bad experiences with automated phone systems.

**Phil:** Given that observation, what suggestions would you give yourself?

**Justin:** I'd tell myself not to be so down on the new system until I've tried it! This one could be different and maybe even better.

**Phil:** Go on, can you say more about that?

**Justin:** Well, I suppose that I've decided the new system won't be effective before I've even seen it.

**Phil:** And?

**Justin:** And I should give it a shot before I make that kind of judgment.

**Phil:** Are you willing to give it a shot?

**Justin:** Ah, yeah, of course.

**Phil:** Justin, I value your opinion and I appreciate your willingness to keep an open mind about this. More importantly your peers see you as a leader; you have a lot of influence with them. What actions can you take to show your commitment to the initiative to your peers?

**Justin:** I'll tell you what—I'll give this initiative 100 percent of my support and effort for the next three months. I'll learn everything there is to know about it, and I'll encourage others to do the same. If our customers are happy and we achieve a five percent increase in customer satisfaction, I'll be happy. But if our customer satisfaction has *not* improved, you're going to hear from me! Is it a deal?

**Manager:** Deal! But I don't want to wait three months, let's check in every few weeks to see how things are going.

**Justin:** Sure thing!

The final step is to **Review the Desired Results** once you start seeing actual results. Compare the two, and with an employee or team, identify and evaluate successes and struggles so they can learn from them. With the individual or team, discuss judgments that held true, actions worth repeating, and any changes that need to be made. It's easy to overlook this step, especially if the results are positive. Great Managers realize that reviewing actual results and how they were achieved is critical in developing employees, creating successful teams, and advancing the organization.

So, here is what that conversation looked like, from a JASPAR perspective:

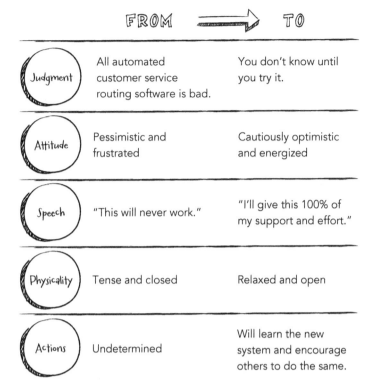

| | FROM | TO |
|---|---|---|
| Judgment | All automated customer service routing software is bad. | You don't know until you try it. |
| Attitude | Pessimistic and frustrated | Cautiously optimistic and energized |
| Speech | "This will never work." | "I'll give this 100% of my support and effort." |
| Physicality | Tense and closed | Relaxed and open |
| Actions | Undetermined | Will learn the new system and encourage others to do the same. |

Now, as you read these scenarios, the manager's questions and replies may not seem like what you'd normally ask or say based on your current training or experience. Perhaps your knee-jerk response to Justin's initially snarky attitude would start with, "Listen, big shot, I don't know who you think you're talking to, but . . ." and devolve from there. However, as a Great Manager, you—and your employees—must shift your thinking and focus to a new paradigm. Rather than *telling* them you don't like their attitude and "this is how it's going to be," engage them and ask about their concerns and attitudes in order to come to a more productive result, as we saw in the example above.

A word of caution: Creating shifts isn't always easy, and it may not happen in every coaching conversation. Managers who are new to coaching may revert to *telling employees* to create immediate change. Having self-confidence is critical at this stage.

Remember that this coaching model is new for you and your employees, so allow time for everyone to get used to the approach and for benefits to take effect.

Here are some additional questions you can use to talk about results:

- What are the results you're getting today (actual results)?
- How have your judgments, attitudes, speech, and physicality created the results you have today?
- What are your desired results?
- What is the gap between your actual results and desired results?
- What about your results excites you most?
- Do you have the tools you need to achieve the desired results?
- How might you look at this lack of results as an opportunity?
- What about your judgments, attitudes, speech, or physicality needs to shift so you can achieve your desired results?

## Worksheet for Chapter 11

## "As Seen on TV!" – RESULTS –
## Desired and Actual

1. What are some of the current gaps between the actual results you're achieving as a manager and your desired results?

2. Have your actions been aligned with your desired results, or are they working in opposition to them?

3. What shifts will you need to make to create your desired results as a manager?

|  | From | To |
|---|---|---|
| Judgment | | |
| Attitude | | |
| Speech | | |
| Physicality | | |
| Actions | | |
| Results | | |

4. For your employees to deliver the desired results, you need to first define those results. Think of a time when you have established the desired results for your employee or team at the outset of a project. What were the actual results? Did they line up with the desired results? Why or why not?

5. Now, think of a time when you didn't clearly establish desired results. How did that lack of clarity affect your employees' or team's performance and actual results?

6. We know that actual results are more likely to mirror desired results when you, as a Great Manager, are deliberate and consistent in aligning your beliefs with your employees' beliefs. Using Powerful Questions from this book, plan a coaching conversation to align your employees or team around the desired results you currently want to achieve.

# Chapter 12

## Coachability

If you're wondering if every coaching conversation will be a success, the answer is no. Building your skills as a coach will help to ensure that you're doing everything in your power to facilitate productive and helpful coaching conversations. However, even your best efforts represent only 50% of a coaching partnership (or less, if you're coaching a team). The success of the coaching conversation depends not only on the ability of the coach, but also the coachability of the employee. As a coach, you'll encounter employees who fall in various places across the coachability spectrum; from uncoachable to highly coachable. Certainly, the more coachable the employee, the more successful your coaching conversations will be.

Both coachable and uncoachable employees hold one thing in common that distinguishes them from each other—desire! For the uncoachable, their desire is to protect and defend their judgments, attitudes, speech, physicality, actions, and results and see things as they've always seen them. For the coachable and highly coachable, their desire is to discover an entirely new set of possibilities. Each employee's desire and the degree of that desire are key determinants of where that person falls on the coachability spectrum.

## COACHABILITY SPECTRUM

Great Managers build a team of employees who *want* to be coached. Evaluate your current employees to understand how coachable they are, and therefore, how likely it is that they will deliver desired results to the business. As your team evolves, consider coachability as a core capability and use it as a standard when deciding whom to hire or promote. The following descriptions will help.

## The Uncoachable Employee

This is the employee who *can* not or *will* not be coached. As a Great Manager, you are destined to have at least one uncoachable employee as a member of your team at some point in your career. The uncoachable employee's negative actions and behaviors are often noticeable to everyone around that person, and their impact can be destructive and far-reaching, negatively influencing other employees, you, your results, and the company.

You may find it difficult to demonstrate support for the uncoachables, as they are likely bringing down others on your team and propelling themselves toward potential failure. Employees who value only their own judgments and have no desire to consider other views may often fail to be contributing members of their teams. As a Great Manager, you will need to manage the influence of the uncoachable on others, the team, and you as a manager. Some people can not be or will not be coached; do not take this as a reflection of your abilities as a manager. Instead, ensure that your team members are focused on the actions they are taking to produce their individual and organizational desired results and not focused on an individual. At the same time, you must support the uncoachable employee by helping that person transition into a role where he or she can contribute best, within your organization or another one.

A word of caution: Take time to assess uncoachability. These people aren't likely to identify themselves with a name badge, blinking arrow, or t-shirt that says "No Coaching Zone." Rather than jump to conclusions, look for these characteristics to be sure an employee is truly uncoachable:

- **They are focused on themselves.** Uncoachable employees have individual agendas that are more important to them than those of the team or company. They may display arrogance, viewing themselves as trailblazers even if that trail isn't leading to the goals needed for everyone to win.

- **They have the right approach but are in the wrong job.** It's an uncoachable situation when an employee believes that *his or her* way is the *best* way, and that the approach just isn't appreciated or adopted because that person is in the wrong role or even the wrong company. Depending on the culture of your organization, you may be able to help this person transition out of the company to a place where he or she will be better suited. Often, uncoachables linger in a company and—like it or not—you'll get your turn at being their manager. If you can't remove the uncoachables from your team or the company, show that person the same respect as any other member of your team. Invest your time wisely, however, and focus on employees who are coachable and are the difference makers in your business.

- **They have no desire to change.** These employees don't want to change their behaviors. They're satisfied with the way they judge the world around them and with their own "right way" of doing things. An employee who doesn't *care* to change doesn't yet have the *ability* to change, so you're wasting your time trying to change that person.

- **They are uncoachable at this time.** An employee may very well be coachable— even highly coachable—but there may be a time, for business or personal reasons, when the desire for change and openness to coaching is out of reach. At such a time, a shift in that person's judgment, attitude, speech, or physicality may be impossible, so postpone your efforts to a better time.

*Here's an example:*

One of the managers in my company, Ian, approached me about his disappointment with one of his most talented employees, Elizabeth. An increasing workload and changing business dynamics had caused her to become disengaged. Her attitude had turned negative, and her actions had begun to impact the team. She started to treat others on the team with disrespect, and Ian believed that it might be time for Elizabeth to exit the company. Elizabeth believed that she was being asked to do the impossible, and she was frustrated.

Ian had several coaching conversations with Elizabeth to talk about her frustration and how her attitude was impacting others. Nothing seemed to change. Elizabeth was defiant and even rude to Ian during their conversations. Elizabeth was showing up late to the office, not carrying her share of work, and had become disconnected from her team. By the time Ian came to me, he had determined that Elizabeth was uncoachable.

I asked Ian to have another conversation to determine if Elizabeth was truly uncoachable, or if she was just uncoachable at that time. I advised Ian to probe a bit more and find out if Elizabeth was focused on herself rather than the business, if she believed that her approach was the right and *only* approach, and if she had any desire to change the current situation.

During Ian's next conversation with Elizabeth, they discovered that Elizabeth was indeed focused on herself and had little interest in the business or her coworkers. She believed that the business approach was wrong and that she was right. However, Elizabeth shocked Ian when she told him that the current situation had to change or she would not be able to continue, and despite everything, she very much wanted to stay with the company. Ian and Elizabeth both discovered that, based on her recognition that things had to change, she *did* have a desire to be coached. With that realization, Elizabeth's attitude shifted—from being angry about the business dynamics to wanting to discuss how things could improve.

Elizabeth now clearly articulated her desire to regain what she had lost, but she was concerned because she needed help doing that in this new business environment. She and Ian both recognized that, during that first coaching conversation, she was venting frustration and had not been open to being coached at that time.

When employees declare themselves to be uncoachable (or you identify them to be so), determine if that's a temporary or permanent state. It may be merely a timing issue, and your efforts to coach at a more approachable time may reap greater benefits. If you're working with an employee who has committed to coaching conversations in the past and is typically open to change, but who seems unwilling at this time, consider asking, "Is this still a good time to talk, or would it be better to continue this conversation later?"

### The Coachable Employee

Coachable employees look for opportunities to improve their performance and work toward team and company goals. They seek out ideas and thoughts of their leaders, managers, and peers. They're curious, ask questions, and are grateful for feedback. They're willing to see any given situation from different angles, and can adjust their judgments as appropriate to pursue a different path or goal from the one they had already set. They're resilient, and they rebound from setbacks stronger than ever.

### Coachability Checklist

When you're assessing an employee's coachability, assume that everyone is coachable until proven otherwise. This checklist may help.

Is this employee:

✔ Making a commitment to coaching conversations and honoring appointment times?

✔ Open to change and creating new possibilities?

✔ Willing to shift their judgments, attitudes, speech, and physicality?

✔ Taking agreed-upon actions as a result of coaching conversations?

✔ Fulfilling promises and commitments made in their coaching conversations?

✔ Speaking openly and honestly with you as their coach?

✔ Building a partnership by providing feedback on what is working or not working inside and outside the coaching conversations?

✔ Getting results from the coaching?

✔ Willing to continue the coaching process?

The more "yes" responses to these questions, the more coachable the employee.

### The Highly Coachable Employee

When you combine motivation with desire, you get the highly coachable employee. As a Great Manager, this is your best coaching partner. In my experience, the highly coachable employee is not necessarily the one with the best skills, the most experience, or the highest education. Actually, the mix of motivation and desire is often better than skill, experience, and education.

In addition to demonstrating the attributes on the coachability checklist, the highly coachable employee will also be motivated to create a vision for their life and work and take action on it.

**Great Managers Know Where to Focus**

One of the biggest mistakes a manager can make is to spend more time on employees who are uncoachable than with those who are coachable or highly coachable. While your good intentions may push you to coach those who seem to need it more and who aren't living up to their potential, you must devote your time and efforts to employees who *are* coachable—because they're the ones who will deliver results.

If you give the majority of your time to the uncoachables, you're depriving those who would benefit most from coaching, such as the employees that value the time they spend with their managers You may even push away the most coachable employees. Great Managers and coaches spend their time coaching those who want to be coached, thus bringing greater benefit to the employee, the team, and the business. Coachable employees can translate the coaching conversation into action. They're willing to take risks, experiment with new ideas, put new ideas into practice, and deliver results for themselves, the team, and the business.

So how will you invest your time? As a Great Manager, your focus should be on employees who are receptive to coaching. Investing in your employees will require your commitment and will include building new skills. In turn, these new skills will make you a Great Manager who can better engage employees and bring out the best in them while achieving the desired results for your business.

## Worksheet for Chapter 12
## Coachability

1. Review the coachability spectrum and the coachability checklist. How would you assess your *own* coachability, and where do *you* fall on the coachability spectrum?

   Now consider your employees and assess who is coachable or highly coachable. Use the coachability checklist to help you through this process.

2. In this chapter, you read about employees with no desire for change. How much time have you spent with employees like this in the past? How much time would you spend with them now?

3. This chapter also stressed that coachable and highly coachable employees are those who need the majority of your coaching time. What commitments can you make to ensure that you'll invest most of your coaching time with this group?

# Chapter 13

## You Can't Fake It

Hopefully, this book has provided you with a good understanding of a coaching model and how to engage your employees in it. At this point, it really comes down to you as the coach. What will you do differently? What are you committed to? Since you've read this far, I believe that you're committed to being a Great Manager. Or you may already *be* a Great Manager on your journey of continuous improvement. Regardless of your motivation, your commitment to improve your skills and engage your employees is commendable!

You can't fake it

The debate about whether Great Managers are born or are taught may never be resolved. However, I'm confident that if you genuinely care about your employees and put what you have learned from this book into practice, you have the potential to be a Great Manager. You can't fake caring, and I don't believe that you can teach people to care about others. Nevertheless, you can certainly teach new skills and capabilities to people who *do* care.

Regardless of the questions you ask or the coaching model you use, the qualities of genuine interest and caring will distinguish you from ordinary managers. Remember that being a Great Manager is not about having all the answers—it's about *asking the right questions.*

223

Making those questions personal and specific to your employees, and asking them with authenticity and care will make *you* a Great Manager.

**Your Investment Pays Off**

> *When you bring the best of yourself to your coaching conversations, you get the best from your employees.*

When you bring the best of yourself to your coaching conversations, you'll get the best from your employees. Your questions will never seem mundane, repetitive, canned, or stale. The more of yourself that you invest in coaching others, the better your ability to ask relevant questions and further help your employees reach their desired results.

Think of a time when you were listening to a family member or good friend talking about a problem or concern. On those occasions, you were talking to a person you cared about, someone with feelings and emotions and fears and goals and hopes for the future. In the same way, a Great Manager considers all those elements in a coaching conversation. Just as you were sincere and probing in that personal situation, a Great Manager is able to get to the heart of an issue and ask Powerful Questions to resolve it and move forward.

By observing your attitude, speech, physicality, and actions, your employees will build a lasting impression of you—and *you* control what that impression will be. Your employees are smart. If you merely go through the motions of asking the Powerful Questions, they will find you insincere, and you will be ineffective.

**The Human Side**
Organizations are focused on building employees' hard skills and capabilities. These are important, but without the softer skills—the

human side of work—you'll never unlock peoples' full potential. Beneath the technical aspects of running a business are the real people we rely on—those who make up our work culture, engage our customers, and execute our strategies. A Great Manager's job is to find the right balance between the soft skills and hard skills. The right balance reflects your willingness and ability to connect with your employees as unique people and coach them to achieve successful individual and business results.

If you expect your employees to reach and exceed company goals, you must demonstrate the type of leadership that encourages their success. We're talking about *your* business, *your* team, and *your* employees.

**You Have the Power**
Will you be a manager who just focuses on operations? Will you be the kind who engages employees only in passing? Or will you be that Great Manager who coaches employees, and thus the business, to success? Your employees depend on your leadership, motivation, and authenticity. They rely on you to listen and ask questions—Powerful Questions! As a Great Manager, you are the centerpiece of the organization. For your employees, you *are* the company.

You are also your employees' direct line to their future. Your employees will remember you for the rest of their lives. Whether you are their first manager or their last, you are leaving an indelible impression. What do you want that impression to be? How would you like to be remembered? What will be your legacy as a manager?

More than just getting through the day, or staffing, or making sure the schedule is right, managing is about people, and about your ability as a Great Manager to bring out the best in them as individuals and as a team. Your investment will ultimately be the single most

> *Your investment will ultimately be the single most important element in the success of your people and the business overall.*

important element in the success of your people and the business overall.

Did you realize you had this much influence? I hope and believe that you'll use your influence in ways that earn the trust and respect of your employees and help them and you to be successful business contributors.

Your success and the success of your employees are inextricably linked. With this knowledge, you can create the relationships that will drive desired results—results that will get you and your employees noticed!

**Your New Path**

You are working on a new chapter as a manager. Don't be shy—tell others that you're developing your skills as a Great Manager and coach. Let your employees know that you want to engage them differently. Identify discussions as coaching conversations. Acknowledge that you're a beginner and that you want feedback. Expect to make mistakes, and value those mistakes as opportunities to learn and improve with each coaching conversation. Be patient as you develop your coaching skills.

You are setting forth on a path to the future of management itself. You are one of the first, and you can be the best. Good luck!